S0-BUA-044

AUDIT LOGIC

AUDIT LOGIC

A Guide to Successful Audits

Philip Kropatkin

A Ronald Press Publication
JOHN WILEY & SONS
New York • Chichester • Brisbane • Toronto • Singapore

Library of Congress Cataloging in Publication Data:

Kropatkin, Philip.
Audit logic

"A Ronald Press publication."
Includes index.
1. Auditing. I. Title.

HF5667.K73 1984 657'.45 84-5192
ISBN 0-471-88403-0

Printed in the United States of America

10 9 8 7 6 5 4 3 2 1

Preface

I've spent more decades than I care to remember in the field of auditing, both in the private and government sectors. In more recent years I was the chief auditor of a large federal department, one that had responsibility for the third largest budget in the world, surpassed only by the national budgets of the United States and the Soviet Union.

During these years I dealt on intimate terms with leaders in the auditing profession (and other disciplines) at many levels of government and private business and with the lively college and university community. Cumulatively, these experiences and contacts enabled me to achieve both a fundamental and a realistic understanding of the underlying philosophy of auditing and how it can best be practiced in our increasingly complex world.

This is a "thinking man's book." It explains the rules of logic that can be used successfully in any audit situation. Auditors need not—and probably should not—depend on canned sets of prescribed audit steps, artificially tabulated to fit minimal levels of coverage generally prescribed by various standards. I have tried to explain why certain thoughtful audit steps are taken, why they should be done in a certain order for maximum effect, and how they all fit together into an understandable mosaic that protects both the auditor and client against material vulnerabilities.

In my experience, those auditors who did rely heavily on, or insisted on, being handed routine audit guides, were at best marginally competent journeymen. On the other hand, those who felt comfortable under any set of circumstances, using primarily their own instincts and understanding, were usually the best performers and potential audit executives. This book is aimed at explaining in an organized fashion how these instincts work and how the logical auditor does a good job and reports the results. Business managers are encouraged to use this book, to better understand how auditors can help their organization and feel more comfortable with their overall process.

PHILIP KROPATKIN

Mill Creek, Washington
May 1984

Acknowledgments

No comprehensive professional book can reasonably be called a solo effort. To a great extent it represents syntheses of everyday give and take with one's colleagues spread over many years. Their thoughts and ideas become, inevitably, a part of one's own thinking. This book is, of course, no exception. Many wonderful friends and talented colleagues gave me their best insights and were responsive to my persistent questioning as to the real essence of good auditing. I was indeed fortunate to be associated with Ed Stepnick and want to thank him especially for his help and wise counsel. I would also like to mention Bob Bergman, Bob Brown, Bob Dias, Hubert "Van" Drooge, Jack Ferris, Phil Majka, Tom Roslewicz, Larry Simmons, Mattie Stern, Joe Vengrin, Bob Wells, and Bill Wilkerson.

My warm thanks go to Neil Tierney, who first encouraged me to write this book. I am particularly grateful to Charlie Johnson for his assistance in reviewing, editing, and providing perceptive, practical contributions to the entire narrative. In addition, I am indebted to Jim Foster for his invaluable assistance in developing the chapters on sampling and computers. As for Bryan Mitchell, his overall encouragement, sage advice, and final review of the finished manuscript are very much appreciated.

I also want to acknowledge the important contribution of Nancy Cates. She took thousands of scribbles and rescribbles, endless inserts and reinserts, and put them all into clear, readable type—a real "pro" with infinite patience.

P.K.

Contents

PART ONE

Introduction

1

Logic: The Main Theme

FINDING THE IDEAL AUDITOR

Ask me what I look for most in an auditor recruit. My answer–a sense of humor! This, I assure you, is no frivolous reply. Consider the attributes of a truly humorous person:

Intelligence (primary).

Interest in, and curiosity about, ideas and things.

Ability to distinguish trivia from the significant.

Articulateness–in writing and in speech.

Knowledge about people and their everyday business and social practices.

All, of course, are essential to those people we consider to be humorful (even comic). Find a recruit with a good sense of humor and you will have a person with the basic characteristics of a truly top-flight auditor.

TRAINING

How to take these intrinsic traits and insights and use them to make a disciplined, independent auditor is what this book is about. One cannot "instruct" anyone on how to be smart. But I think we can translate and transform native or inherited intelligence into professional expertise that is both practical and reliable.

THE AUDIT ARENA

Good auditing involves a step-by-step process that can be subdivided in a number of different ways and given various labels. Labeling provides a handy framework to study and discuss the techniques and, equally important, the thinking processes inherent in the performance of audits—any audit!

One method of useful subdivision calls for following the timing of each phase of an audit and then discussing what is involved in the performance of each level of the examination. Fleshing out each phase, in a time sequence, probably makes the most sense since auditing any business, or government entity (a public business), when done well, is actually performed in a certain order. There is a necessary rhythm to the process.

A possible scenario, in brief, runs like this: (1) Identify the audit target and client; (2) decide on the scope and audit period; (3) survey the audit entity (perhaps the least understood yet the most important phase); (4) evaluate the survey results and prepare an audit guide; (5) complete the audit steps; and (6) relate what was found to the scope and decide what was found to be right and what was found to be wrong (summation). Naturally, the verification or the checking of details in a disciplined fashion is an ever-present part of the entire process.

In discussing these generally divisible stages of each audit, I will cover a variety of new techniques, a refinement of old techniques, and different methodologies that can beef up the reliability of each audit—while holding down precious staff time. I will be generous with helpful hints and shortcuts!

I am convinced that good audits are *disciplined exercises in controlled logic*. This approach ensures that end products (audit reports) will be practical blueprints of what needs fixing (operations and procedures), prospectively, and a reliable opinion of what needs adjusting (financial statements), retroactively.

This book is intended to be a sophisticated primer to aid the truly modern auditor. A "primer" since it deals with fundamental audit principles (or logic). It looks into new ways of returning to and coping with all of the basics, reexamines the fundamental checking and listening (e.g., auditing) techniques, and discusses how we can lower our analytical common denominators—making them all workable in the new business world, where traditional audit trails are growing thinner. The book is "sophisticated" in that it attempts to analyze and discuss these basics in new or ingenious ways that will be useful to the modern examiner of internal business practices—at any level (from student to managing executive).

It should be helpful whether the auditor is on the payroll of any large or small business (for profit or not), a practitioner in any size CPA firm, or a staff member of any audit group representing various city, state, or federal agencies. Logical audit processes are intrinsic to all audit situations. Advanced students will discover that the ideas that follow will give them a running start in their drive to become able and reliable practitioners in an increasingly complex business and social environment.

Things aren't static. There should be little doubt that our social, business, and physical environments are becoming vastly more intricate and difficult to cope with. The widespread use of electronic transfers of funds and records and the disappearance of "hard" documentation create increasing opportunities (and appetites) for abusive practices that are harder and harder to uncover. We may have no visible checks in a few years, no written interoffice memos by 1990, no paper at all by 2000! This prospect puts added professional strain on the people assigned to certify by their examination of business processes that all is well.

SHORT SUMMARY OF EACH CHAPTER

I have stressed that there are readily divisible parts of the audit process. Let me refer you to the section "Main Phase of Audit," where I've summarized and interpreted them for your ready reference. You will see how strongly I feel that a good, well-planned survey is the keystone of audit work. Poor surveys result in wasted time and reauditing; they misfire evey time!

Part Two goes further into the preliminary stages of the audit. Many of the points made here may strike the experienced practitioner as elementary. But here I ask only that these experts reflect a moment on their experiences when they were fledglings or consider the needs of the fledglings on their staff. Indeed, many of these obvious points are too often overlooked.

I believe that you will like Chapter 3, "Thirty-Nine Steps, or How to Visualize Starting and Finishing an Audit without Skipping a Beat." I sought suggestions from other practitioners for appropriate items for this checklist and, even now, am puzzled as to how many of the salient points were overlooked by true experts in the field. So "before you start your engines" for your next assignment, gentlemen and ladies, review your checklist.

In Part Three, "Survey: Forming the Important Tentative Audit Opinions," you will find what I believe are some rather important observations on just what you should be thinking about as you perform this keystone portion of your audit. The subheadings assigned to this part give a foretaste of my line of thinking.

A Logical Approach. Chapter 4 covers preparation of a survey audit guide. This essential road map, so often (actually, most often) skipped must be developed to ensure that you look at all of the steps you review. You will find some insights as to how to proceed and illustrations of survey methods that are easily adaptable to most audit situations.

Bad Vibes, Good Vibes. You are probably familiar with how it feels to look at something that doesn't exactly displease you but that raises a mental red flag. Chapter 5 contains illustrations of this type of situation.

The Clues Must Fit. Additional examples of "red flag" situations are described here. Such situations can be glossed over by the novice auditor, or the pragmatist, but they can (upon analyses) reveal situations that are real corkers!

Mental Auditing, or, What Could Go Wrong? Chapter 7 expands the discussion of situations from my own experience of ways in which the auditor must constantly consider how abusive situations can be fostered by a client's operations and result in serious damage.

In Part Four, "Verification: Extending the Survey Results," you will find a comprehensive, succinct explanation of sampling for modern auditing: underlying logic and practical techniques. There are just two basic types of sampling. We are all well aware of judgmental sampling, a good technique that is useful in situations where it is called for. An example would be pulling and examining every 10th voucher. Probability sampling (known also as statistical or scientific sampling) is simply a technique that the practitioner should be familiar with in practice and comfortable in discussing. I've made no attempt to overwhelm the reader with infinite detail and formulas but have confined myself to presenting basic insights into this valued technique. I suggest that you first study the point sheet for this part before proceeding with the text.

The real theme of Chapter 9, "Computer Auditing," is that you cannot do a good job of computer auditing (or managing computer auditors) unless YOU understand–thoroughly understand–computers. Simply stated, checking security methods, operating controls, programs, transactions, and the like cannot be left to the technicians. Let me note that this is one of the few instances where I believe that the auditor must be particularly skilled in a technical area under audit. It cannot be audited around or left to specialized computer wizards. The text illustrates the scope of this fantastic technology, using actual case examples to demonstrate how vulnerable a computer-based organization can be to sizeable theft. I believe that the auditor who understands computers by combining classic audit techniques with the important concept of "compartmentalization" will be able to make a truly professional review of any ADP operation.

It would be hard to picture anyone but the most ardent dieter who would turn down fresh rolls at breakfast; "Stale Rolls" just aren't the same. Chapter 10 uses this simple theme to illustrate the problems encountered if auditors fall into the quicksand of auditing stale transactions. The critical concept of on-line audits—the what must be present, and what must be done factors—is discussed here, also.

Traditionally, auditors have concentrated on "inputs," management processes, functional controls, administrative practices, and the like. But changes are underway, as discussed in Chapter 11. Auditors are now beginning to gauge "results" against "expectations" and are thus assessing the accomplishment of business objectives. Sophisticated data gathering methods are a must, as are proper criteria by which to judge results. The making of a profit is not a guarantee per se that all is well. (Perhaps larger profits were possible!)

The title of Chapter 12, "Cost Accounting—Easy Does It," is particularly descriptive. The chapter puts this very important area in its proper perspective to make it less overwhelming, especially for the new practitioner. While accounting for cost is a complex process, understanding some of the underlying concepts is relatively easy. This section spells out the simple logic underlying all cost accounting applications that can be put to good use when needed.

All of us at one time or another have come to the end of the day with the feeling that we have not accomplished a thing. Many swings but no hits—the time was wasted. I've never believed this since it has been my feeling that some good comes out of every effort (I couldn't find that widget at any of the stores visited, but at least I now know where *not* to look). This simple idea points up a problem that often perplexes today's auditors—the assessment of basic research, particularly when the only end product is a research report. Chapter 13 "The No-Product Dilemma," explains some fairly simple and useful steps that the practitioner can take to perform a creditable review in the area of auditing basic research projects.

It is certainly nothing new that fraud and situations conducive to fraud exist everywhere. Chapter 14 illustrates some of the more prevalent types that each of us without knowing are subject to on a daily basis. Auditors face implied and mandated responsibilities in this tough arena. The discussion covers traditional and modern techniques that can be used in this continuing and growing struggle. In the computer age, the abuses may be very material, and therefore of direct concern to all auditors.

The how-to of summation (that is, writing an audit report) as discussed in Part Five represents a lifetime of study and thinking on my part. I have dissected this troublesome task into three chapters: 15, "Writing the Finding," 16, "Summaries" (or comparing the good to the bad), 17, "Recommendations" directed to just the right layer of managerial action.

As you read through this entire text you will find that I urge you to become expert or knowledgeable in quite a few important areas. But, as I am sure you know, the ability to communicate your thoughts, observations, conclusions, and recommendations on the printed page is a valuable asset too many auditors lack. Simply stated, you learn to write well by writing, by studying the writings of good writers, and by knowing your subject matter well. Ask any top executive what, more than any other attribute, brings one person to the top faster than their competitors, and they will often agree on the ability to communicate well. Good technicians abound. But effective communicators are rare!

Is the typical bright young graduate accountant a ready-made auditor candidate? Unfortunately, my reply must be a resounding no! Chapter 18, "Why Auditors Should Be Only Part Accountant," examines why the present educational background of an accounting-trained auditor candidate just is not sufficient. (As an important aside, let me say that in addition to an accounting background, attributes such as being interested in what makes things tick also help distinguish between good and mediocre audit staff.) Given the educational deficiencies that exist, audit groups must provide the wherewithal to effectively educate new recruits in audit matters not covered in their college accounting curriculm. And, of course, such continuing education is also necessary for all other professional staff to ensure that they too are current in the skills and requirements demanded by their particular work. A case example is included showing how such a training program was implemented for a large, typical audit organization.

The final chapter discusses, dissects, and interprets auditing standards promulgated by the AICPA, the General Accounting Office, and the Institute of Internal Auditors. It not only ends with a discussion of the standards that auditors must adhere to, but it compares and provides concise, thoughtful (mystery-free) overviews of just what these standards involve. One cannot really adhere to audit standards without understanding audit logic—what this book is all about.

THE MAIN PHASES OF AUDIT

Description and Discussion

The auditor should appreciate that while the principal parts of the audit require applications of somewhat different techniques, the handling of each audit segment must fall into a cohesive, rhythmic pattern to be most effective and efficient, as a whole effort.

At the beginning of the pattern is the "preliminary stage."

The Preliminary Stage

Here the scope and purpose of the review is pinpointed and delineated. (Is it a systems study, a financial attestation, a fraud examination, a compliance test, or any combination of the above?)

Many audits that fail, misfire right at the outset. They do not properly perceive who the client is, what he wants, nor what is essentially needed. Consider straight financial audits, sometimes called the "Attest Function." Does the balance sheet accurately depict the assets and liabilities of a specific business entity, at a given moment in time (December 31, 19XX, etc.)? Also, why did the net equity change from one year to the next? A profit—or loss?

The Survey

This phase requires the auditor's best judgment. He or she must decide what looks strong, what appears weak. The overall operations of the internal controls must be evaluated. The hardest decisions in the entire audit usually are made right here. For an audit to be cost effective, the auditor must stick with these decisions unless glaring new disclosures dictate change later on. Constant comparisons must be made in the auditor's mind between expected norms and initial observations. The full audit guide is usually best developed at this stage to test all the *initial* opinions formulated at this time.

Verification

This term means exactly what it implies—a evidential check on tentative conclusions—no more, no less.

The Summation

The summation, where findings are narrated and put together concisely and where recommendations are presented for corrective action (or adjustments made to ledger accounts), is believed by many practitioners to be the most difficult. Understanding the proper technique of report narration will probably take most of the "sting" out of this process. Writing cannot be left to the so-called language wizards. They cannot—and should not—refine, develop, and express your thinking for you.

Finally, an audit is not finished until the auditor takes full advantage of the lessons learned on every assignment and tucks them away for the next job or as a follow-up to the past assignment. This is an intrinsic part of the continuing education of an auditor and cannot be minimized. It closes the loop.

Cementing the whole process together is the certification by the auditor that all his or her work was done in conformity with the profession's standards of conduct and technique. Auditing is both an orderly and immensely interesting process. The almost infinite variety of matters to deal with and the constantly changing conditions are fascinating and continually challenging.

PART TWO

The Preliminary Stage: Establishing Scope and Purpose

2

Prelims versus Main Event

AN OVERVIEW

Preliminaries: what does this word really mean? To a boxing or other sports fan, it signifies the matches or events that take place before the main event is presented. They are intended to flesh out (an appropriate phrase) the full program. They do not directly influence the main attraction, nor do they form an integral part of it. Furthermore, they generally are not part of the business arrangements preceding the star attraction, which is independent of them in a professional and athletic sense. Most certainly, the "prelims" are not an intrinsic preamble to the *judging process* of the main event. The results of the main events are not influenced by the actions in preliminary bouts. Also, dull or exciting prelims don't necessarily mean uninteresting or spectacular finals.

In auditing, however, it's all different! Preliminaries are not detachable from the main effort. They *are* critical to its success and *do* affect it in fundamental ways. We can expect therefore that the resolution of recommended actions should be a natural continuation of the prelims, not a separate part of the program. Here, then, is the general scenario that illustrates this entire performance.

AUDIT PRELIMINARIES

The prime purpose of audit preliminaries is to precisely fix what the main object of the review is and determine who called for the review in the first place and orchestrated its performance. The "who" can be a specific or discrete client, a corporate or management official, an elected official representing the public at large, or even a state or federal judge. The "what" is mainly an administrative process—one that responds to some formality. For instance, publicly held corporations are required to be CPA audited every year, and nonprofit recipients of public funds must have their records audited no less than biannually. Audits can even be called for by private clients who want assurances of good internal control and information on how economical and efficient a firm's operations are.

SETTING THE SCOPE

Determining the complete scope of any examination has to reflect both the purpose and audit objectives of the specific organization under review. It should *not* be a pro forma, boiler-plate, or check-list exercise. It certainly should not be fully delineated or decided by the chief auditor until the survey is finished, at least. Why? The internal survey controls may appear so weak or the potential for abuse so great that an extended audit scope is obviously called for.

If the survey is the working blueprint for what is needed in the verification process, then the scope should be the actual description of what the full parameters of the audit are and what important steps should be taken to get there from the initial starting point.

In any case, audit preliminaries should not be glossed over; they are important to the overall success of the main event. They set the stage for defining the scope; they influence the arrangements for and the staging of the survey and the verification of the survey analyses; and lastly, they indirectly lead to the performance of the main event itself—which is, of course, a report with appropriate recommendations for corrective action or prospective change from the previous year as a result of either a profit or loss from the year's operations. Obviously, you must also ensure that you have the proper staff, at the right place, at the right time with all the knowledge it can bring with it from prior audits. This is compatible with internal and external audit standards, which call for all auditors, before they start, to bring to all audits related field work, education, and experience; independence; the formality of an assignment; planning; and sufficient resources.

In the attestation audit the client (or corporate officers) want an independent statement of the firm's financial position for several reasons, but usually to reassure third parties. This type of audit does not by itself—should not and probably cannot—consider whether the client's operations are economical or efficient. This type of review is usually called an operational audit; it attempts to disclose whether the business practices of the past year were expeditiously done or could have been done better. Whether the firm should have been doing this type of work in the first place is also not a part of the balance sheet audit; nor whether the intended results of the institution's business aims were achieved or not (results-oriented review). The pattern of succeedng with audit actions depends primarily on deciding in this opening stage what needs to be done and how extensive the examination process will be.

SURVEY

The next stage is where the all-important tentative opinions regarding the entire enterprise are formed. The evaluation of survey results and the preparation of specific audit guides for the engagement is insufficiently recognized as one of the most important phases of any audit and the hardest to do right in a cost-effective manner. A full discussion later on is devoted to this crucial audit phase.

THE MAIN EVENT

The performance of the remainder of the audit (based on the results of the survey), otherwise called the *verification process*, may be deemed to be the centerpiece of this book. Various old and new techniques will be discussed in depth.

You will get a new look at sampling and a very different approach to and insight into computer audit methods and "matches" of related computer-stored data. There is a discussion of an important technique called "on-line auditing." All of these techniques must be integrated and tied into other audit methods—interviews, analyses of performance data, and physical observations. All clues must fit! (Fitting clues together is given its own separate treatment.)

THE SUMMATION PROCESS

The summation—what was right or wrong, and its impact—is yet another essential area. The "summing up" process is probably the hardest of all for the auditor and/or his or her supervisor and manager. Summing up takes many forms during the course of the audit, including (1) individual workpaper conclusions, (2) status briefings on audit progress, and (3) individual findings, financial analyses, and/or even full, comprehensive reports. All are difficult to do right. The shorter they are, the harder it is to maintain the correct balance. But none is considered effective if it does not in the briefest form possible accurately compare "what was" with "what should have been."

The final end product—the audit report—must maintain a proper relationship to the scope of the audit. It is essential to let the reader know what the audit found in relation to what the auditors set out to seek. Consider it as reporting on deviations from a bench mark. Audit reports should be practical blueprints of what needs fixing (operations and procedures), prospectively, and reliable opinions of what needs adjusting (financial statements), retroactively. It is absolutely wrong to depend on oral briefings to clarify, or supplement, what should have been crystal clear in the auditor's final written report.

POINT SHEET

PRELIMINARY STAGE

Prime Purposes of Audit Preliminaries are as follows.

Precisely fix "what" the main object of a review is. Is it

- An attest function?
- A performance audit?
- A compliance check?
- A hostile examination?
- A special internal review?

Determine "who" has called for the event.

Remember that audits are usually requested in response to some formality.

- Publicly held corporations are required to be audited by a CPA every year.
- Non-Profit recipients of public funds must have biennial audits.
- Private clients want operational assurances.

Preliminaries cannot be treated lightly; they are important to the main event.

They set the stage for the definition of the audit's scope, for the survey, and for subsequent verification.

Each audit is discrete and requires a unique set of preliminaries; all require planning.

Preplanning consists of having proper staff with adequate education, experience, independence, and prestudy of related work or prior audits (all normal "standards" for internal and external audits).

Some helpful "starters"

Obtain related prior materials.

Reports.
Permanent files.
Previous working papers.
Tax returns.
Related legal files.
(lawsuits, corporate minutes, stock registry, etc.).

Assemble similar industry analyses.
Many are publicly available.
Many comparable audit reports of related companies are useful.

3

Thirty-Nine Steps, or How to Visualize Starting and Finishing an Audit without Skipping a Beat

This chapter is intended to be a handy and complete outline in miniature of all the important steps that should be taken by an auditor to start, manage, and finish any audit. The opening gun is, of course, the assignment, or initial engagement that calls for the performance of a specified audit. The final salvo will, generally, be an audit report containing a set of audit recommendations for corrective action. These suggestions are the end product of the whole production even—and this is critical to the logic of the whole audit sequence—even if the auditor sees no need for material change and recommends that operations be generally continued in the same manner as before.

This qualification follows the old Boston adage, "Don't try to make good better." Though it could happen in actual practice, I must confess it rarely does, especially in a large, diverse, or complex business, or in a loosely formed government institution.

Nevertheless, in some respects the underlying thought is very similar to that made in Part Three on surveys; that is, don't spend unnecessary audit time on procedures or practices that are well done or at least very satisfactorily performed. Similarly, don't encumber the final audit report with trivia or unimportant recommendations. Save these for short oral briefings, supplemental advisory letters, or a memorandum of minor findings. Use any informal communicative device that suits you and the client or any other interested parties. By any standards the value of the audit report is not (should not be) thought of as being based on the number of findings that are presented with long lists of related recommendations. The success consists of balanced summary statements showing how much went well and what needs fixing.

The following steps should be viewed as handy memory joggers for field practitioners. They are not intended to be all inclusive. They are grouped under the classic four main stages of the audit—preliminaries, survey, verification, and summation. This breakout serves as a useful road map on the way to a successful audit.

PRELIMINARY PHASE

1. Get a fix on the precise nature of the assignment and the desired end product.

   For example, does the audit on attestation function need a correct balance sheet and profit and loss statement, for public or other use?

   Other objectives could be a performance audit, stressing the efficacy of the operations; a compliance check, designed to see if the entity is doing what it was paid or commissioned to perform; a hostile examination, designed to determine if certain actions, fraudulent or otherwise, occurred (this audit usually involves legal outside authority); a specialized internal review, designed to answer whether inventorying techniques are satisfactory or computer security sufficient, and so on.

2. Obtain related audit reports, permanent files, previous working papers, tax returns, and like historical information. Also, follow up on actions taken on prior audit recommendations, as a prerequisite to your audit. If actions were not taken, ascertain why. If actions were taken, inquire or determine whether they achieved the desired impact. Perhaps something else remains to be done. If actions taken were something other than what was recommended by the prior audit, did these alternate actions achieve the desired effect in the minds of management?
3. Get industry analyses of other publicly available summaries or reports on the auditee, any related organization, or subdivision.
4. Establish tentative time perimeters for this assignment. These can be changed if conditions warrant, but don't leave the question of time open ended.
5. Determine what staff resources are sufficient to do this job fully, based on your best estimates.
6. Hold an entrance conference with the auditee and lay out mutually agreed-to audit objectives and target completion dates. These should be embodied in an acceptable engagement letter, if appropriate.
7. Request initial working data from auditee for preliminary study (A/R, A/P reconciliations, inventory tabulation, corporate policy and operating manuals, fixed-asset details, insurance policies, pending legal actions, organizational charts, procedural flow charts) and other like matters. Get a positive fix on all ADP equipment, all pertinent ADP programs, and related data banks. This is critical! The details needed will depend on the size and complexity of your client's business.
8. Reserve adequate staff working space and secure commitments for computer time and for responsive secretarial

and duplicating services. This should be arranged with senior auditee officials and not be left to working-level office managers. It is more important than you think!

9. Prepare a *survey guide* that will serve as a broad-based working road map for the staff auditors to follow based on the preliminary data gathered and the individual characteristics of this particular audit entity. The guide will minimize missing or skimping on important preliminary coverage steps.

SURVEY PHASE

10. Physically inspect and/or observe the entire organization such as warehouse(s), plant(s) and equipment, office layout, real and personal property, computer room, filing system, receiving and shipping area. Stay alert during this process. Don't be hurried through it by bored or impatient auditee personnel.

11. Compare your observations of physical items to the paper records of the organization. Do the recorded fixed assets, for example, look like the "real" plant and equipment?

    Review the parts and the whole of the managerial information system and appraise the process from a conceptual point of view. Consider whether the operating reports appear to be:

    Designed to disclose operations and problems to management.

    Promptly used by managers to formulate decisions, change policy requirements, and take action on identified problems and not just used for "compliance" or "for show" paper trails.

12. Determine (and this is most important of all) whether all the processes and functions logically relate to the physi-

cal aspects previously observed. The clues must all fit. An organizational chart, for example, with numbers of people in each segment should correspond to the general impression absorbed by direct observation of what the staff looks like. Some rather elemental items can be easily missed. For example, if the Comptroller's Office shows 65 people on the payroll, did you see them on your physical tour? How many time cards were there on the wall? What does the internal telephone book show? (Office personnel usually have their own telephone on their desks.)

13. Prepare flow charts for process and organizational understanding. They need not be especially detailed and may even be preferable if short and to the point. Flow charts following specific tests should be made and those tentatively deemed weak should be verified later and expanded, if necessary, to determine the full extent of the weakness (material or trivial; too much, too little).

14. Pay strict attention to cash—count petty cash; reconcile bank statements after cutoff arrangements have been made; check internal controls over receipts. Remember, cash is a vulnerable asset.

15. Scrutinize accounts receivable, accounts payable, and other balance sheet and profit and loss items. Analyze and note the oddities or extremes in entries during the entire year.

16. Consider plant operations—how about

Tools. Inventory them and consider how they are expensed.

Resources for depreciation. Recompute the depreciation for accuracy.

Hazards and related insurance.

Security, both assets and paper records.

Efficiency indicators. This is just a reminder; whole libraries are filled with suggestions.

Cleanliness, one key to the extent of managerial control.

17. Consider the keepers of the books. Who are they? What is the internal control factor, who do they respond to and who hires, rewards, and fires them? Watch for intercompany transfer items. (Keep in mind the important distinction between administrative controls and accounting practices. See Part Six on standards, where this point is mentioned further.)

18. Check any union arrangements–talk to the labor representatives of the company and the union. What about pension policies and funds? Wrongful acts frequently occur in this area.

19. Keep in mind the critical question, What could go wrong? Be reminded of the AICPA Standards' statement with regard to the auditor's basic responsibilities: "Auditors must do *whatever* [emphasis added] is necessary to detect gross errors or gross misapplications." Therefore, the question of what is potentially and seriously damaging is obviously of great concern. And, adapting this type of questioning as a frame of mind throughout the audit is a healthy attribute. Probably the best suggestion is to visualize and try to work out (like solving an intellectual puzzle) how you could "take" or "rip off" this organization if you wanted to–alone, collusively, from the inside, or with the help of suppliers, buyers, or visitors from any quarter.

20. Take appropriate samples–short acceptance takes, or full-blown projectable samples. (See my entire Chapter 8 on this most interesting subject affecting almost every aspect of the auditing cycle.)

21. Determine what is being tested before taking any sample. The sample universe has to be homogenous and "clean."

22. Decide–and this is more easily said than done–why the object of the testing is being tested.

23. Decide *precisely* what would constitute an error. Make sure, also, that the universe is clean, in which case this step becomes much more definitive.

24. Consider what will be done with the test results. Will such results culminate in a meaningful recommendation?

25. Study and know (conceptually) the important difference between probability samples and judgment samples and how each can be drawn (procedurally) with reliable results. (See Part Four for a fuller discussion.)

Probability is another word for predictability. Any probability sample is valid at a given confidence level. Samples of 200 or more will likely be sustained by the courts for dollar adjustments between parties. Scientific predicates need a good clean universe (if not, stratify the sample population until clean). For random selections, precise agreed-upon terms as to what is an error or not are very important. This repeats point 23 for emphasis. Consider the distinct relationship to quality control mechanisms in this whole process.

Remember that judgmental (nonprobability sampling) is more subtle, not fully scientific, harder to defend, but very useful if done right. Under controlled circumstances a sample of one may be valid—to prove a point. Similarly, a "fishing around" sample may be reliable if interpreted correctly. For evidentiary purposes, fraud cases may need only a judgmental sample of one. Nonprobability sampling can be very useful in discerning a trend or "feel" for the siutation. It can be combined with probability samples or a stop-and-go technique that consists of incremental short samples.

26. Remember, too, there are three main averages: (1) measures of dispersion, (2) normal distribution, and (3) probability distribution. The arithmetic mean, loosely, is the division of the sum of a given set of values by number of values. Be careful, though; it's "pulled" in the direction of—that is, strongly affected by—extreme values. The median or middle value is less affected by any extremes. The mode, the "most prevalent" value, tells which item came up more than any other. (That's all it does.)

27. Consider how dispersion should be mathematically calculated and used to measure the reliability of an average. It shows the relative spread and gives insight into the extremes. These extremes may also govern the selection of a particular type of sample. Simply put, dispersion is the variation in the data being studied and describes the significance of differences in the data field. It can be used to measure the reliability of an average. In mathematical terms, it's called the "standard deviation." There are other gauges—like the "range," which is the difference between the largest and smallest values. But range doesn't give useful information about the dispersion of the intervening values. The standard deviation overcomes this objection.

A normal distribution is simply the old familiar bell-shaped curve. If the universe under study is normal, then valid inferences can be drawn from the curve. For example, we can tell the percentage of items within a specified distance from the mean. If the universe is not normal, then special handling is required—better stratification, for instance.

Probability distribution is defined as a listing of possible outcomes of the sample and the probability of occurrence for each outcome. The two main classes are binomial and normal. Binomial probability distributions have only two categories—like heads or tails—each independent of the other. Those that are normal have an infinite number of outcomes in the experiment.

28. Consider the use of computer cross-matching for a 100 percent sweep of any automated data. Computer matches can be considered to be a phase and an integral part of the sampling process. If properly thought out and constructed, the computer match sweeps out every result that falls outside of the auditor-directed parameters, without exception. The auditor can then examine all the aberrances or, if very numerous sample them for subsequent close-in scrutiny of tracts or elements for whatever results or purposes the auditor had originally contemplated when he programmed the match. This powerful process is more explicitly described in Chapter 9.

29. Stay on top of training needs. Every auditor should attend various training courses, in school and on the job, and engage in enough self-study to stay knowledgeable about the following sampling techniques, their weaknesses and strengths, and when they should and should not be applied:

Unrestricted samples

Stratified samples

Cluster samples

Acceptance samples

Discovery samples

Interval samples

Dollar Unit samples

30. Don't audit around the computer. The same basic logic should be applied to this modern arena as to the more prosaic "tic-and-holler" school of auditing. The logic is the same, but the manner of applying it must, of course, be much more sophisticated and modernized.

The first step, and probably the most helpful over the long run, is not to take a certain step; that is, don't take the lazy man's route and look for computer wizards to evaluate internal controls when fulfilling audit responsibilities.

31. Check computer security. This is easier said than done. You can keep your head above water most times in this very rough sea if you apply the "compartmentalization" test to basic situations. That is, there must be constant separation between process control and physical hardware. This control distinction must be present at *all times* for adequate internal control to be effective.

32. Know how to use computer matches to assist in unlocking aberrant postings or entries in any combined, comparative, or interlocking set of records. Use my handy memory jogger, "Komputer Karate"—the force of the target computer turned on itself.

33. Don't be overwhelmed by cost accounting assignments. This is a separable subject in the audit thinking process in many ways. Again: don't let it throw you; it's easier than it seems at first. The clue is to look if the system estimates sensibly, based on prior experience; adds overhead on a sensible basis; has a method for checking itself; readjusts on a timely basis; keeps accurate books, learns by its own history; does not mix apples and oranges.

34. Stay alert to the possibilities for fraud and abuse. Here are some sobering thoughts on this ugly aspect of our business society combined with a few generally useful and sensible suggestions:

There is real cause for audit concern, because in our modern society one finds

Extensive cheating (a national art form)
Widespread shoplifting
EDP vulnerability (hundreds of millions of household computers to think about)
Tax evasion on the rise
Drug and medical practice abuses
Counterfeiting made easy with modern duplicating techniques
Misleading advertising everywhere, which fuels a general attitude of nontruth
Very uneven reprisal or punishments for wrongdoers

Consider the above at all times in the context of the auditor's overall responsibilities and standards of achievement. Understand the basic composition of a possible fraudulent situation. If an individual has sufficient motive and opportunities for real gain, there is strong reason to suspect fraud. The higher the stakes, the greater the motive to overcome workable deterrents. The market in illegal drugs is a good example of this principle. For further illustration let me just merely list an agenda of 15 items from a typical training conference held last year for a national audience.

Assessing controls in electronic funds transfer systems
Internal auditors and the deterrence of fraud
Combatting the great employee benefits fraud game
A case study in comprehensive fraud investigation
Coupons, redemptions, and fulfillments: or, opportunities to be clipped
Fraud investigation: Is there a role for the internal auditor?
Selling, establishing, and operating corporate policies pertaining to fraudulent activities
Fraud in construction and government contracts
Procedures for containing white collar crime in the procurement process
Thefts and fraud in the oil patch
The world (or is it galaxy?) of computer abuse: Can auditors cope?
Data security controls—protecting the information resource
Dealing effectively with law enforcement and prosecution
Using computer audit software and microcomputers for fraud investigation
Rapid growth and business difficulty: Examining the climate for management fraud

To summarize, all auditors must adhere to the general terms of the profession's standards for guidance. As to the fundamental question—should the independent auditor be held responsible if his or her ordinary examination of financial statements fails to detect a material fraud—the answer is clearly yes, when such failure results from noncompliance with generally accepted auditing standards.

35. Sharpen your reporting skills. The main thought to consider is that the principles and techniques of accurate narrative and reliable conclusions developed by the auditor are the same no matter what the composition of the reporting media, which can include:

A comprehensive report, combining analyses, other reports, trends, series of other reports, etc.

A single report summarizing findings, usually of a single organizaion or subject

A summary of a single report

Findings

A summary of a finding

A briefing memo

A curt executive note

All of these written products will suffer if they do not display careful, short, and interesting handling of the English language. Above all, do not mislead the reader by intent or maldesign. The reader must know what you think is important and why (and how to deal with it) and what is of lesser concern.

36. Make recommendations fit the report and the reader. Who will act on them and how? The answer to this question usually represents the culmination of the auditor's responsibilities for the audit.

37. Carefully "staff" your findings during the entire course of the audit to ensure accuracy, understanding, and psychological (and emotional) acceptance by every level of management affected. This relates to item 35 above, Recommendations. Keep in mind, no surprises! Talk to managers about your findings. Unless they are hiding abuses, most will welcome intelligent suggestions that honestly consider the practicalities of the business problem at hand.

38. Make sure you get replies that are responsive to the matters recommended or reported. Do not take this for granted. Insist that they be timely. It is too late to deal with them back in the office with overworked supervisors making needed patches to the report. Don't indulge in any self-delusions about getting apparent concurrences.

39. Have an explanatory exit conference. If there are any surprises at this meeting, either management's bringing up new evidence or the audit executive's springing new conclusions, the basic audit process broke down somewhere in the entire cycle.

POINT SHEET

39 STEPS

1. Get a "fix" on the assignment—balance sheet audit, performance audit, compliance check, internal review, etc.
2. Obtain related material, reports, tax returns, previous work papers.
3. Study industry analyses of related organizations.
4. Set time budgets. Change them later if needed (and warranted).
5. Get commitments of adequate staff resources (as prescribed by standards).
6. Hold an entrance conference to set mutual objectives.
7. Have the auditee help with preliminary working data (A/R, A/P reconciliations, prior inventories, ADP equipment and operating data, etc.)
8. Get a senior client commitment for administrative support.
9. Prepare a survey guide to ensure full audit coverage.
10. Physically inspect the entire organization.
11. Relate (mentally) physical characteristics to basic records (people, equipment, etc.)
12. Correlate steps 10 and 11 with organizational and process flow charts. (Keep it simple for a bird's eye understanding.)

13. Set up a series of survey tests to tentatively decide on strong and weak points.
14. Pay strict attention to cash, the most vulnerable of all assets. Be careful, especially if working under ADP processes.
15. Scrutinize other balance sheet and profit and loss items (A/R, A/P, cost of sales, etc.). Analyze them for extremes and material aberrances. (Remember, nothing happens in an organization all by itself)
16. Scrutinize plant operations for hazards, security, obvious inefficiences, cleanliness, etc. These are useful clues.
17. Always carefully check internal controls, keeping in mind the very important distinction between administrative controls (urgent) and accounting practices (less vulnerability).
18. Check union arrangements, pension funds, etc.
19. Keep in mind "what could go wrong." An auditor must be able to spot gross misapplications.
20. Know sampling distinctions–acceptance, (for surveys), probability (for settlement purposes).
21. Sample only a homogenous (clean) universe.
22. Decide (before sampling) why something is being tested.
23. Decide what would be an error (before sampling).
24. Determine how the sample will be used.
25. Be able to scientifically distinguish between probability and judgment samples.
26. Study averages and what they mean (or purport to mean).
27. Understand dispersion and distribution concepts.
28. Use the strength of the computer itself to pry open key aberrances from auditee's computer data through the technique of computer matches (a form of computer karate).
29. Insist on extensive staff training in sampling and computer operations.
30. Do not leave computer auditing to "computer wizards" who don't know audit logic.
31. Check computer security–look for "compartmentalization", the separation of *physical* and administrative processes.
32. Match computer results to other material disclosed in the full audit process.
33. Don't be overwhelmed by cost accounting auditing and conceptualization. Extensive prestudy is inefficient; each case is different.
34. Stay alert to fraud–the ugly spectre. It takes many forms and is of great concern to management and to auditors.

35. Sharpen your reporting skills. Reports are the real end product of an audit. Clearly written reports won't mislead the reader in any way.

36. Aim recommendations correctly. Describe who takes corrective action and how.

37. For staff findings at all levels, abide by the old adage: no surprises.

38. Get responsive replies. Make sure they are clear and make sure whether there are concurrences or not.

39. Have a frank exit conference, necessary insurance for auditee and auditor.

PART THREE

Survey: Forming the Important Tentative Audit Opinions

4

Logical Approach

Let me stress again: The survey technique is considered by many—including this author—to be at the very heart of any audit or review process. It entails every bit of training, understanding, and ingenuity needed for a successful and cost-effective audit. The verification phase, performed later, is really the more precise proving ground that tests and develops the tentative audit conclusions drawn from the critical surveying (or scanning) of the clients' entire bookkeeping and overall physical plant operations. Again, as in every part of the audit effort, an orchestrated rhythm or tempo should be established to make the survey reliable, complete, and disciplined so that the auditor can do it in the least time possible and with optimum results.

STEPS IN PROCESS

To start this whole proces properly, one must first clearly fix the audit objectives firmly in place. Every member of the team, especially the leader, should know what the end product is meant to be. Is it to be a full attestation of the balance sheet and profit and loss statement? Usually at the top of the popularity list, this classic audit effort goes back, in primitive form, to the Biblical era—probably even earlier. The "keeping of accounts" is almost timeless. In modern terms, it basically involves the taking of an accurate snapshot of all the items owned (or owed) by the client on a given day and translated into monetary units. Called a balance sheet, it usually is accompanied by an explanation why last year's snapshot has changed (the profit and loss statement). How to do this right is, of course, the most traditional and formally studied and described of all the audit endeavors. Whole libraries exist to codify and explain the extensive ritual auditors must perform (in massive, excruciating detail) to be able to certify that this instantaneous view is accurate, also that it is in keeping with agreed-upon accounting principles and auditing standards, and that it is in perfect focus, meaning no fuzzy items clinging to the operations that could be material but are not clearly identified. Examples include large pending lawsuits, other contingencies from tax reviews, or other hostile situations.

The balance sheet does not validate an opinion as to whether the business ownership made as much money as it should have (with the equity it had) or was as expeditious and efficient as it could have been (with the existing work force), or spent as little as possible to accomplish its objective without getting into unnecessary sideshows. It does not offer any opinion as to present or future operational vulnerabilities in the business, like computer security, inventory and special tool controls, or even unnecessary fire and theft hazards. Above all, the balance sheet attestation does not, in most cases, establish, in a truly practical sense, the real-world commercial net worth of a business as a salable commodity. Chapter 6, "Clues Must Fit," explains this important concept more fully.

STRATEGY CONSIDERATIONS

I would like to describe in some detail the underlying strategy that is intrinsic to any well-performed survey, how interesting it can be, and how important it really is, as a managerial process, in audits of any sort.

Again, the first consideration for the auditor is to clearly understand what type of audit is called for. Next, the auditor must prepare a survey audit guide. This essential road map will serve to ensure a step-by-step analysis of all the various elements of the business that need preparatory audit attention. This surely should be done before one attempts to write a sensible audit verification guide. The basic factors are indeed elementary, but deciding how to evaluate them is vastly more complicated. The survey results, as a self-standing entity, should enable the auditor to have a positive feeling of what is likely to be correct and reliable and what is possibly or probably weak and erroneous, what can be left as done and what needs deeper audit penetration. How easily said! How hard to do!

But back to the survey guide. It should essentially serve like a handy tickler guide to remind the auditor to be orderly in his initial analyses, as it leads him through the process.

PREREQUISITES

As a good beginning, the auditor should analyze the starting, and recorded, financial statements; the budget; the various departmental cost analyses; accounts receivable and their aging; cash flow; and any accounts payables (also aged)—comparing all these figures one year to another. Changes, trends, aberrations, (even unbroken continuations) are important. The size and the dimension of the entire operation are there to see. So are the number of people on the payroll and the real property descriptions. Many, if not most, of the essential clues to needed further auditing are all there. Many verification steps can be considered, to a great extent, to be extensions of analyses of the financial statements that can, as a good start, be analyzed in the auditor's own office before the examination begins.

LEG WORK (WEAR GOOD SHOES)

Next come physical observations, marching down the road checking matters piece by piece. The ability to relate what one sees in the physical sense to the financial books makes them more meaningful and is a potent source of audit insight. For example, how extensive are the administrative offices (how many rooms)? How big is the manufacturing plant? Subplants? What is a real working shop, what is dormant? If the office looks small and there is a large payroll on record, where are the people (or vice versa)? If the plant has a lot of heavy and bulky equipment, is it on the books? Is it equipment that can be productive for the plant's operation? If it looks old or heavily used, do the depreciation records match its real value? What about related insurance coverage and outsiders' assessments?

The survey guide will call for an examination of correspondence and secured papers, such as securities, leases, insurance policies, corporate minutes, tax returns, and so on. Many important audit clues reside there. One important caution comes to mind here. Don't be put off by any manager who takes a position such as this: "Tell me what you're looking for and I'll show you precisely what you want." You really don't know, at this point, what you (*precisely*) want. Key interviews with executives, managers, and the working force at all levels must be fully utilized. Flow charts are a must for understanding and sorting out who does what and who controls whom in the whole operation. Let me branch off at this point and show, by analogy, how one might conceptualize a logically well-performed survey.

Do We Plod, Meander, or Plot Our Observations?

Several years ago there was an international furniture fair in Frankfort, Germany. This exposition featured different styles and makes of furniture from all over the world and demonstrated the particular appeal of teak and oak as opposed to various metals and plastics. There were also many combinative creations, of course, all with the special flavor of the originating country and its creative designers. It was a large, zesty exposition, housed in a huge horseshoe-shaped building, with about 35 separately furnished rooms. All were on one level, with informal cafes, shelves of literature, and naturally, sales booths clustered in the center area.

While spending the better part of a day there, I was struck by the different approach taken by various spectators from different countries, individually and in family groups. Three essentially different methods of observation were evident.

One family was mechanical and plodding in its approach. It mathematically divided its viewing time (let's say 6 hours, or 360 minutes) into 36 essentially equal segments, allocating 10 minutes for each and every room. There seemed to be no room for flexibility. No distinction seemed to be made between what interested the family members or what bored them. They started at room no. 1 and worked their way around the horseshoe, one by one, room by room, until they had methodically finished viewing the entire showroom. They seemed determined to get their money's worth.

Type two was more erratic. People in this group started out essentially the same way, going straight to the first room to the left of the horseshoe entrance. Only they were very haphazard in their approach—15 minutes at room 1 (routine), 5 minutes at room 2 (no interest), 45 minutes at room 5 (fascinated)! This group rarely got beyond the 10th room.

Type three was my favorite kind of viewer, employing sensible and useful survey tactics. These people would enter the showrooms at the left, trot around the entire fair, obviously making overall mental notes of what attracted or repelled them and what especially interested them. After this all-inclusive, quick "survey," they would then return only to the specific showrooms that were of more than routine interest and that in their minds merited detailed verification. This can, of course, be compared to the classic auditor's preferred survey technique.

Don't Be Bashful

Look around; talk to key people. Come right out and ask office managers, plant foremen, or operating executives (or even the sales force) what are the problems they perceive and why they have not been (or could not be) solved yet.

Their answers will in most cases be forthright and sincere. It is not disloyal to the company. After all, except for hostile engagements for special reasons, the auditor generally is looked on as a potent, perceptive agent for potential improvement. Take short acceptance or judgment samples of document groupings. Test various internal controls; confirm payables and receivables; perform some test inventories, and so forth. Then, go back to the "hot" items.

SENIOR STAFF INVOLVEMENT

Although I am digressing somewhat, I wish to make one more point concerning surveys, since they are really the most important part of the audit cycle. But all too often this critical process is left mostly to relatively junior personnel. Senior audit managers frequently set the audit in motion, make personnel assignments, and then generally, and in only superficial terms, discuss with the assigned staff the audit approach, strategy, and end-product expectations. These managers usually and dutifully attend entrance conferences at the auditee site. Then they also leave the actual survey work, involving the sensitive judgment calls regarding close-in audit approaches, or the selecting or discarding of potential areas for deeper scrutiny, to less perceptive, certainly less experienced, and usually less well-informed audit personnel. All wrong!

A potential homeowner would be pretty upset, for example, if he found that a journeyman plumber, a good bricklayer, and an experienced carpenter were constructing their dream home while the architect and supervisory engineer who drafted up the general plans came along once in a while, later, only to look things over and see how they were going.

Audit managers often find themselves, as a result of this slipshod practice, reviewing poorly done audits after they are finished, sometimes desperately trying to paste together and patch up missing elements in the draft conclusions. Often, auditors-in-charge must sheepishly return to the auditee for more backup information. Worse yet, they might have an audit report later disavowed because of inaccurate evidence or erroneous recommendations.

THOSE TENATIVE OPINIONS

But back to the survey. After doing all the steps mentioned to this point, auditors must form tentative opinions as to which procedures are strong and which are weak. They should spend the rest of the audit extending the tests—with probability sampling—concentrating audit time in the weak areas only; determining the exact extent of error or weakness and the probable causes. They should not plod through and routinely verify the entire set of books and records (allocating precisely 10 minutes to each and every "showroom" without distinction as to materiality, vulnerability, or relative importance).

Let me now further emphasize my next point because I consider it absolutely vital to a successful and economically performed audit. A survey should, in itself, be the *action-forcing prelude* to each of the critical steps in the verification process.

The verification phase should be designed (and carried out), after the samples, interviews, observations, lateral connections, and so on, merely and pointedly, to verify the survey results. There is no logical or economical reason to retest what was already deemed to be strong. Auditors must steel themselves to respect their own judgment. Of course, they must learn how to take the smallest risk possible; but doesn't every review, investigation, analysis, evaluation (yes, the whole audit) represent a relative risk in the entire assessment process? Of course it does.

THE BENCHMARK DEVELOPMENT PROCESS

Here is yet another way of looking at this tension between comprehensiveness and careful targeting. Underneath it all, there should be a logical thinking process that a good auditor arms himself with before he ever starts the audit assignment. The process begins with what one might call a working pre-image of the business or operation under review—a benchmark or a preset mental standard. What the auditor must form in his own mind, in almost every phase of the examination, is a business picture of what would constitute good performance were he to see it. How many receiving documents out of how great a total must be accurate for him to consider this to be a reliable part of the operation? Regarding accounts receivables and accounts payable, how many errors will he tolerate in this business before he considers the controls to be substandard and meriting deeper investigation. The mental image the auditor has of what would constitute good performance must be performed before the start of the survey audit.

If, for example, you are sending out independent confirmations for the very important accounts receivable verification, how many errors would make you wary about the entire process—1, 5, 50? But remember that the overall total number of customer receivables is not a determining factor. (Remember probability sampling.) Also, the stratification of the accounts is relevant—how many are big, how many small. This feature, of course, should affect your sample. A major customer with a very large account (outside the sample) reporting an error of some consequence does raise serious questions to a much greater degree than do a few normal-looking, incidental customer errors of low dollar amounts inherent in the basic sample plan. But the point is, where (before you get the results in) in your mind is the dividing point? Take a stand! That's what they pay you for, to know how to do this.

CALLING MR. HOLMES

One further point, relative to the whole survey technique—the clues must fit! Don't discount or dismiss facts that are not fully and rationally explainable. This is how you miss frauds or major weaknesses. All the clues must fit. Let me cite some examples, some from actual experiences, some constructed out of my own experienced imagination. The value of the first type is self-evident; these cases are instructive because they actually happened. The latter cases, perhaps to an even greater degree, are important because they could happen. Isn't this another example of one of my major themes—a good auditor can, and should, visualize, and frequently anticipate, all possibilities of error, abuse, aberrant practices, and the innumerable ways that things can go wrong, inadvertantly or deliberately. Therefore, if one can "manufacture" a case study in this clues-must-fit context, it is a real sign of having understood good auditing instincts. Also the reader should be aware that auditors—good auditors—bring all facets of their life to bear on their work. The perceptive integration of their training, their private experiences, their extensive reading, their exposure to all the various thoughts and processes that go on in both the business and the social world will enable them to react intelligently to almost any situation in real-life auditing.

Anomalies or discordances, things that don't fit, should (will, if done right) pop out and present targets of opportunity for the auditor to pursue in audits at any level, in any entity, whether private or governmental.

The logic of audit perception should prevail no matter what. It exists, for instance, at the core of all good writing involving mysteries: spy stories in which specific clues are used by detectives to solve cases. Perhaps the most famous of all time were the Sherlock Holmes mysteries. Old pipe-smoking Holmes would take one very remote or esoteric clue and build entire personalities and life situations around it. Modern day writers do the same thing. And they all work, for the main part, backwards. Let me illustrate.

A writer will pick up a notation or an idea, and then weave a whole characterization into that instance. A perceptive writer will observe, for example, that left-handed people and right-handed people tie their shoe laces differently. Every animal, humans included, have a special side orientation. (Even snakes will tend to coil to one side or another.)

Now the writer puts the reader (or the viewer of a movie, or TV screen) in the position where they only see the tail end of an incident. Let's say it's a murder. The body is fully dressed. Everything points to a certain suspect—motive, availability, witness, various circumstantial evidence, documents that are indiscretely written, and so on. All clues seemed to fit and point to one suspect.

However, one of the facts that comes out in the investigation is that the victim's body was found fully dressed in an athletic locker room wearing a warm-up suit and sneakers. The detective noticed that something was wrong with the way the laces were tied on the sneakers. He didn't say so publicly at first, because he didn't want to tip his hand. But he put the clue aside because the bows were tied on the wrong side of the foot. The victim was a lefty, but the bows were tied by someone who was right-handed. Hire that detective—he's a good auditor! The discrepancy led the detective to the tentative (survey) conclusion that somebody put the shoes on the body after the person was dead and didn't pay attention to which side the bows were on. The right-handed murderer or his accomplice put the shoes on the dead body as he would have put them on his own feet, with the bows pointing, let's say, to the outside right.

This simple clue that did not fit was just one of 99 others that did. A case easily could have been made to indict the wrong suspect because of the 100 clues, all pointed to him except this one. The detective was not satisfied. And he should not have been. The one clue that did not fit negated the rest of the profile.

Similarly, an auditor should not be satisfied with one seeming insignificant clue that does not fit. It may throw doubt on all the others, making them null and void. I will get back to some specific real-life examples of how this works in the audit business.

First, because of its importance, let me develop the theme, if you will, a bit further. Everybody loves to solve riddles. Only in most cases the riddles we hear are sort of children's pasttimes where a silly question is asked, like why did the chicken cross the road? And the silly answer is, of course, to buy a home in the next county where the taxes are lower. If you want to respond to adult riddles or, better yet, if you want to compose them, the way to do so is to start with the clues that don't fit or with the clues that do fit, but in an odd fashion. Better yet, starting with the item itself, the object of your riddle, itemize crazy clues that do and do not fit and see if the reader can sort them out and solve it.

It should be obvious that it is much easier to make up riddles than solve them. But here are some good examples. A riddle poser can, for example, look at his own thumbnail and say, hey, this would be a good subject for a riddle. Why? A number of reasons. Thumbnails are everyday objects. Almost everybody has two. They always move in one direction. This is an intriguing clue. It can be shown scientifically that thumbnails move constantly, all the time, very slowly, with some variations, depending on the sex of the person, the time of the year, and the humidity of the area they live in—they travel at about .017 millioneth of a mile an hour, up and down. Now, there's a set of really zesty clues. You can pose the question, What moves at such and such a rate, always in one direction, as your thumbnails do, and can be found in billions of places (wherever people are)?

Clues that really fit only one thing make up the theme used in most spy stories. Spy stories use one key clue as a fulcrum, around which a large part of the drama is constructed. The writer knows the central clue really doesn't fit any other situation. And the hero (detective or secret agent) knows, too. If he can only figure out its why and wherefore. The writer works out the clue or the set of clues first, in his mind, and then proceeds from there to build the entire story.

The real-life audit business is analogous because the same logic prevails. Auditors have a fundamental responsibility to do what is necessary on each engagement to ensure that no material oversights take place. The best means to this goal is to pay attention to the clues and make sure they fit a cohesive, rational pattern.

POINT SHEET

SURVEY

Surveys (The Heart of the Entire Review Process)

Successful, cost-effective audits depend on good surveys.

The verification phase is the proving ground for the tentative audit opinions formed in the survey.

Reliably done surveys require an orchestrated, disciplined process.

Steps in the Process (Strategy)

Clearly fix the audit objectives firmly into place.

Every member of the team (especially the leader or the auditor-in-charge) should know what the desired end product is meant to be.

The most common end product is the classic balance sheet and profit and loss attestation, (in the private sector).

In the public sector, the most frequent audits are the financial management audit and compliance tests of grants and contracts.

Prepare an audit guide to keep track of the important things to cover in the survey. It is an essential road map for the survey audit team.

Examples of things to cover in the guide are: comparisons with previous financial statements and budgets to identify important trends; departmental cost analysis; accounts receivable aging; payroll; real property listings; securities held; corporation minutes; physical observations of insurance coverage (or gaps), local tax return, flow charts, and test inventories; organized interviews. (There are many good encyclopedic audit texts that will cover these in great detail.)

Who Should Actually Perform the Survey (Technique)

The survey ought to be performed (or at least actively participated in) by senior personnel and not be delegated to relatively junior staff members—very important!

All the regular routine workpaper preparation routines and controls should be observed.

Timeliness is very important:

Relate this portion to the general concept of looking at current (on-line) transactions.

Also tie the negative aspects of late work and the use of junior personnel to the "Stale Rolls Syndrome" (see Part Four, Chapter 10). Senior managers (presumably the best on staff) end up massaging old reports or conclusions reached by lesser-informed or experienced personnel, with no time left for the new assignments and timely supervision on the job.

Results of the Survey (Decision Time)

Those parts of the clients' system and operations showing strong internal controls and those aspects of business that are working well should be left alone.

Weak points should receive the bulk of subsequent audit verification attention; verify the survey results (the main objective).

Results should also be compared to the auditors' *present* criteria (what he would consider to be a good operation, were he to see it).

Above all, the clues must fit in the overall survey assessment.

Final overall results lead logically into the next audit phase–verification–which will use full-blown samples for extrapolation, etc.

Survey Techniques Right from the Heart of the Standards

Many of the judgments made by the auditor in the survey stage, where the audit really starts, influence the choice of what to more deeply test or what to quickly accept.

5

Bad Vibes, Good Vibes

This chapter is written primarily for the purpose of alerting auditors to the usefulness—well, let's say more accurately, the necessity—of sharp and beady-eyed observation during every stage of the examination. Alertness, one of the key attributes expected of an auditor, is not solely an inherited trait but involves acquired skills that can be honed and sharpened by practice, if not just by steady attentiveness.

Now, one might think up dozens, hundreds, maybe thousands of examples (if one queried sufficient friendly sources) to illustrate this theme. Here are a handful of my own.

During any audit engagement when you find that a certain thing is happening, you should instinctively make a tentative, initial judgment as to how it strikes you. I maintain that each and every encounter should give you a positive audit vibe or a negative one. Neutrality and nonattentiveness are not productive. To best illustrate this broad point, let me construct some situations. Some are real, some contrived. They are not listed in any special order, but only as they came to mind—or as they might be encountered in an audit.

Example 1. Management's written (or verbal) policies and manuals are drafted by knowledgeable employees but either not finished or constantly under revision. All the same, there seems to be a clear desire on the part of upper and middle management to make these the best possible directives. Bad vibes! Chances are management, as earnest as it appears, does not have a clear and consistent, internal executive viewpoint of what its main operational objectives are and what techniques it will actively pursue, employ, aggressively defend, or even tolerate, to get there. Conditions to look for are:

Bad employer-union personnel relations. Personnel with grievances or complaints will have no policy to relate to.

Vacillating marketing and selling methods; poor procurement methods, maybe even uneconomical everyday buying that misses available discounts; promises of deliveries that cannot be met, etc. (Ask to see the correspondence files for customer accounts.)

Poor recruiting results (cannot decide whether to buy talent, train talent, steal talent, etc.). The firm is probably experiencing a high turnover of upper middle and executive personnel.

An unhealthy reliance on the general counsel and his or her office for decisions that should be dealt with by the executive staff.

Example 2. Office personnel often huddle and consult in groups over some knotty problems concerning how to post, allocate, or handle certain groups of documents that are out of the ordinary and require special supervisory attention. Real earnestness by workers and their chief seems quite evident. Bad vibes, Especially if this is an older established office. The company's workforce should know by now how to do things. Fairly good vibes, if it is a newly organized group honestly trying to get things right. In an older business what might appear to be concientious discussions often stem from never cleared-up instructions, poor underlying accounting procedures, uncertain processing of paper flow and, in most cases, inexperienced office managers or computer technicians in over their heads in an expanding business.

What to look for:

Mispostings, mostly in the company's favor (just to clear items and get them out of someone's hair).

Charges to the wrong customer or in error to the right customer.

A backlog of uncleared actions.

Unnecessary gambles on new accounting methods or quick-fix computer systems (an undue urge to start "afresh" and clean up murky operations).

Example 3. Supervisors or executives (senior or junior), who cheerfully insist on being personally helpful, steer you through the intricacies of the accounting system, the detailed (probably unnecessarily complicated) cost allocation systems, and the reconciliation of general summary accounts to various detailed items. They provide explanations of the special transfer or holding accounts that are a "little tricky" or need complicated handling because this company is unique and "unlike anything you ever saw." Bad vibes! The system should be able to speak for itself, in almost all cases. If it needs individualized explanation, then it might be kept, manipulated, or used for inappropriate purposes—known or unknown to the top executives, or behind the scenes (stockholder) ownership.

You should look for:

A patchwork system held together by personalized "stitchery."

Temporary (or permanent) fund complications.

Numberous interbank, intercompany, or interbranch transfers.

Tax or liability evasion, or inaccurate deferrals.

Outright fraud or aberrant practices.

Example 4. Factory stations or service maintenance sites are methodically and fastidiously (almost fanatically) cleaned up each and every night before the entire work force is dismissed. Time is taken to see to it that every tool is systematically put back in its own designated spot. Good vibes! Even though this may, on the surface, seem like a supervisor's or boss's obsession with fastidiousness or unneeded and uneconomical tidy-up practices, the neatness urge almost always evidences a good, well-managed, and conscientious operation.

What to look for:

Only very minor tool losses.

Reliable mechanical work and high customer acceptance.

Good morale.

Timely production of work orders and an orderly flow of cost accounting or project orders.

More examples follow.

The office manager works late most nights. Bad vibes! The question should be obvious–what for?

The office or production manager insists on taking the auditor to "really good restaurants" *every* lunch time during the course of the engagement. "They may take a little longer, but it's worth it." If this does not give the auditor bad vibes, he or she should try another profession.

One of the key policymakers in the organization has a "folksy" office cluttered with plants, recent newspaper clippings, magazine articles from all over the country, lots of books–some on very esoteric subjects–frequent phone interruptions, etc. My vote here is for good vibes! The need here is for a thinking Renaissance man, not one merely responsible for controlling paperwork or tightening production.

Warehousemen who work very hard at cleaning up and repackaging damaged but repairable major line items in their area. Bad vibes! Be extra careful in situations like these. Don't be dulled by the surface (and laudable) sincerity of employees' fixing bad items. Ask why the item was rusty or leaking in the first place. You may find, for example, as I once did, that 8,000 expensive outdoor kitchen kits were being methodically ruined by, of all things, a leaking fire extinguisher that had been placed in each kit as a conservative safety addition!

A restaurant has regular customers who insist on always sitting at "their booth," and will only have certain preferred waiters serve them because of their quickness and especially friendly service. Bad vibes! Desirable customers come regularly to the same restaurants for the good food, at a price they can afford; not for the special waiters. These preferred customers may be getting "preferred" lowered checks from their waiters, who then get extra tips from the customers who specially ask for them.

A department store section manager has upward sales totals when the trend in almost all the other sections is down. He claims that more aggressive and effective selling in his section and extra customer attention are paying off. Bad vibes! It is unlikely one department head can buck the general store trend. He may be artificially stimulating customer appeal and sales totals by lowering prices on sale slips without recording each markdown and sending them by the accounting department. This will be found out eventually because the only way to cover this up on a long-term basis is with subsequent inaccurate physical inventories. But the short-term harm will be very difficult to detect.

The head chef in a bustling restaurant personally takes the time to check most of the meat, fish, and grocery deliveries for accuracy of weight, correctness of order, and quality of merchandise. Mixed vibes! He could be in "cahoots" with suppliers; but he also may be just a nut about superfresh incoming food.

Trash removers on an outside contract are utterly reliable—come rain or shine, snow or hail—they appear and almost never with any substitute personnel. They want this account badly for their cash flow and are willing to beat any and all opposition on price. Bad vibes! They may be removing more than trash or garbage from the client's establishment. (Trash removers pay low wages and are hardly ever *that* reliable.

You are the auditor in charge of a year-end examination of a large steel fabrication plant. The firm's controller assigns you and your assistants to a very small working office near the main steel cutting warehouse, explaining that this enables you to have the privacy you need without disrupting crucial office operations. Besides, you will be very near the plant operations. What should be your reaction? Mixed vibes, mostly on the negative side. This is not a small organization. The controller can easily move some of his clerical personnel out of their offices to accommodate you for a relatively short while. Besides, he must know that most of your work will entail close scrutiny of his recordkeeping operation—more so than the time spent in plant scrutiny and observation. Why is he denying you intimate access to the bookkeeping force?

A large multibranched retail chain organization with a very well-organized, tight accounting system seems to have a rather high advertising expense, considering the conservative nature of the firm. Expense vouchers and related cash disbursements check out and seem to be in order. When you mention this anomaly to the vice president (treasurer) during the annual audit, he replies that he personally looks into operational details in some instances. He happened to have checked into these expenses on his own and found them to be okay. Bad vibes!

Why was the vice president, a senior executive of a large company, personally checking advertising bills? This situation has all the earmarks of improper involvement or a coverup.

While you are auditing a large modern hospital, you observe the procedures employed in the incoming new patient area. They seem very efficient and up to date. Each patient's history is quickly recorded on a computer terminal that provides an automatic printout. The extent of the details recorded seems quite adequate and comprehensive without being overdetailed or redundant. One repeat patient, however, who happens to be checking in, comments that the last time he was admitted (just 6 months ago) this same information was submitted and recorded—like his mother's maiden name, his social security number, previous illnesses, and so forth. The admitting clerk was patient and polite, but explained that a new patient updating for each admittance was hospital policy and insured absolute accuracy and currency of data.

Mixed vibes! I would wonder why the admitting clerk couldn't get a previous admitting record and profile and merely update it. Look for a possible inability of the hospital to routinely and quickly retrieve patient's complete medical data, x-rays, lab tests, and so on. Medical data and trend information may be distorted because of an overworked or inadequate retrieval system.

During the course of surveying the operations of a county's maintenance operations (snow removal, road upkeep, sewage, water district, safety control, etc.) you interview one of the division chiefs. In the course of the conversation you suggest (softly, politely, and encouragingly, which is the best technique for this purpose) that you would like to visit some of the field stations. Maybe one he (or she) considers best for comparison purposes and another one at the other end of the performance rope. The division chief thinks he readily knows all his station's weak and strong points. To be honest and cooperative, he suggest dropping in on station xzy, which would serve both your purpose and his since he has not had a chance to visit them recently. Bad vibes!

If he knows that station xyz is relatively weak, he should find the time to be there *more* often than the others. Don't be misled by his candor and seeming intimate knowledge of his own divisions. Look for other stations that may be even worse than his infrequently visited site. Maybe the ones he gets to visit often are really his main concern.

A senior vice president in charge of production at a multilocation manufacturing organization informs you during preliminary orientation discussions (you are the senior on-the-job auditor) that his (or her) plant superintendents are all excellent and superconscientious. He recalls few if any instances when he put in a call to one of his plant chiefs, at practically any hour, and they weren't almost immediately available to respond to him. Moreover, they could always answer his inquiries, no matter how detailed they were. Bad vibes on a number of fronts!

First, nobody is that good. Second, the plant chiefs were obviously on an unnecessarily short tether apparently responding to the immature management style of the "boss." And finally, wouldn't one reasonably expect the plant managers to periodically be out on the floor looking at operations, first hand, and talking to workers and foremen personally?

POINT SHEET

Alertness Should Be Strong Attribute of Good Auditor	Results from A combination of traits, some inherited, others developed through practice. Attentiveness is important.
All Audit Situations Should Result in a Positive or Negative "Vibration"	A Few Bad Vibes Policy manuals never finished. No grievance mechanism. Vacillating marketing methods. Unmet deliveries. High turnover. Accounting processes never firm. Intercompany fund transfers. Too many late workers. Long lunch hours.

Some sales sections out of line with others.

Undue executive involvement with relatively trivial details.

A Few Good Vibes

Clean maintenance of factory station areas.

Policymakers (as opposed to the doers in an organization) have offices cluttered with reference material.

Second-tier executives occasionally taking time to personally check some details on their own.

6

The Clues Must Fit

Let me now expand on this interesting prescription.

CASE NO. 1. Some years back I was examining the efficiency and reliability of a large-scale warehousing and depot operation. The client had from 12 to 15 enormous warehouses as much as a quarter of a mile long with railroad sidings nearby and stocked with heavy-duty merchandise in gross packaging for shipment on call when warehouse instructions were received.

In the course of this examination, I walked through all the warehouses from one end to the other and made the following observations. Overall, the warehouses looked clean, dry, and properly ventilated. They looked firm—there were no sagging piles or any signs of deterioration among any of the goods. I was especially concerned about some of the cardboard containers, which tend to get crushed or to deteriorate even if only slightly wet. Also, they could be subjected to rodent infestation and other animal abuse. The merchandise itself was orderly; identifications looked clean. The same merchandise groupings were all kept together wherever possible. It seemed like a nice warehouse operation from that point of view. I had also previously checked into the bookkeeping for shipments. I looked at the files to see if there were customer complaints about late, broken, or inaccurate shipments, but could find none. It seemed like a good operation.

Previous inventories had disclosed a minimum of errors. The monthly partial inventories taken on an on-line basis were recorded properly, properly sampled, and attested to and verified by members of my staff on a very timely basis.

The railroad sidings looked appropriate. The tracks were in an orderly condition. It seemed those cars that were there were being loaded and unloaded without undue delay so that there would be no charges for railroad cars sitting on the lot.

I had also noticed company policies called for systematic checking of railroad cars and other vehicles entering and being dispatched. All in all I was satisfied with the entire operation.

But one thing stuck in my mind. There was the usual number of warehousemen in and about the plant—just enough to do the job. I noticed, however, that in one warehouse there was a group of three or four men working on something in the aisle on something like a footlocker full of equipment. I had passed by them earlier in the day and said hello. I asked them what they were doing, and they said they were repairing the contents of one package—an apparently normal thing to do. But by the end of the day, that clue did not fit, in my mind.

If the operation was as good as I thought it was, why did two major containers need maintenance and repacking. What was the trouble? I walked back to satisfy my curiosity about this item, a footlocker-sized container full of kitchen parts that were used by large groups camping out in a field who needed a portable full-sized kitchen. It contained a small knock-down primus stove and a set of basic cooking utensils for a dozen or so people—ladles, knives, sharpeners, and various kitchen accoutrements. They were all heavily rusted. I asked one of the men why they were rusted. He said well, he couldn't be sure—they weren't all that bad—but it took about a day's work to clean up these kits. I said, "kits?" That opened my ears. "Do you have more of these boxes that are rusted and need maintenance?" He said, "Oh, sure! Almost every one of them." "Every one of them?" I asked. "How many do you have?"

He said, "Well, we have about 8,000 here." I said, "8,000? How much does each one cost?" His answer was, "about $320."

I said, "they are all spoiled?" He wasn't sure; they were opening the boxes one by one, but he thought they were all spoiled. The men all agreed. They seemed to have a rather large continuing workload here that didn't seem to bother them much. They were scraping the rust off and coating each piece again with a light mineral oil so it would be reusable, and packing it up again.

I looked at the packaging again. The whole kit was sealed and with a heavy flexible aluminum padding that was airtight, they said. If the packages were airtight, why would they be rusting? They couldn't figure it out. It must be that air was seeping in. Even if it would seep in, it wouldn't rust the utensils. The warehouse was dry and everything else was free from wetness (sounds like an advertising slogan).

I looked more closely into the kit. Included in the spare parts was a small fire extinguisher kit (about the size of a folding umbrella), that contained carbon tetrachloride for oil and other similar fires. Then an interesting thought struck me. Maybe this fire extinguisher was the source of the trouble. Had they considered that? They said, "no."

"Isn't it possible that the fire extinguisher is leaking inside this airtight kit, causing the chemical fumes that are far worse than oxygen in the air to corrode these parts?" That question opened their eyes a little bit. They had not thought about that possibility.

Looking at fire extinguishers, you really could not tell whether they were leaking. I took one and examined it closely on the back, where it was written that it must be replaced every 3 or 4 years because some slight seepage would occur after the first couple of years. Not long thereafter, the fire extinguisher would become inoperable.

Then, I carried a couple of extinguishers from open kits down to the fire station, checked with the fire chief, and asked him about the nature of these fire extinguishers. He said, "Oh sure, these have to be replaced every once in a while; otherwise, they tend to run out and cannot be used. They become nonfunctioning."

"Is it possible that their fumes would become very corrosive?" "Oh, yes, quite possible." Sure enough, upon further checking and rechecking with some experts, they were the culprit. These simple fire extinguishers—meant to be a safety device and placed in every one of the airtight kits (airtight to prevent moisture corrosion)—were systematically destroying kits, one by one. Almost $20 million worth of kits were being methodically ruined. It would have gone on forever, despite the fact that they were opening them up on a long-range work basis, one by one, to fix them up and rehabilitate the entire stock. Upon being resealed, these would have then corroded once again and then again, forever, except for the fact that "the clues didn't fit." Why were they scrubbing up a box of parts in an otherwise beautifully run warehouse operation?

CASE NO. 2. This example concerns a refuse, paper, and cardboard collection place. The company serviced large office buildings, picking up the trash every day and bringing it over to its warehouse. Workmen sorted it out, tied up all the soft paper like magazines and newspapers, and bundled those up; then took out the cardboard containers which were worth more money, sorted them, and tied them into large crates. And anything else like metal goods or bottles was put into other containers and disposed of at normal trash pickup points by the city.

It was a dirty operation, I must admit—but nevertheless, it was a profitable one for a family-run business. It was also hazardous to a certain extent. Workers were dealing with all kinds of merchandise, with tough machinery that baled and bound up the paper crates, paper cartons, and cardboard containers with bailing wire, and so on. It was not unusual for minor injuries to occur among the workmen and family members who pitched in during the heavy-duty times.

Insurance was a big item of overhead expense. In checking through the insurance payments, the policies all seemed appropriate; they were normal; the coverage was adequate for the risks that were involved for injury, theft, and so forth. A number of vehicles were maintained, and the building itself had to be safeguarded—a large building with offices and so on.

The premium charges on the books were all in keeping with the bills that were submitted. The independent broker whom I saw on occasion at the office seemed adept at his business in understanding the insurance needs of the organization in full, including life insurance necessary for business continuity as well as liability insurance of the appropriate kind. But all the clues didn't fit.

One thought occurred to me during the course of the last quarterly audit review. How come, I asked myself, there were never any rebates from the company. In an operation as large as this one with as many insurance complications and changes in policy coverages and changes in company rates, considering the nature of the business, there must have been at least a few premium changes and rebates that would accrue to the company from time to time. There was not a single record of one rebate that I could find in the books of record. I contacted the insurance companies directly, and sure enough, they had a whole slew of changes and rebates due the company that had been sent directly to the company's independent insurance agent. The agent, it turned out, was merely pocketing the rebates and paying all of the gross charges from lists that the company had made out.

The single clue that didn't fit was the single omission of a single recorded premium rebate.

CASE NO. 3. The third case involved a large steel fabrication plant. Production included steel plates, girders, I-beams, H-beams, and so on. An ancillary operation was scrap steel. Single entrepreneurs from all over the county and further would come in every day with truckloads of scrap steel, which would be weighed in with a full truckload. The drivers would then dump their loads in a pile in the open yard, turn around, and be weighed in with the truck empty, the difference represented the tonnage of miscellaneous scrap steel, for which they would be paid so much per pound in cash right on the spot. Of course, special items in the scrap, such as batteries, that contained more expensive metals of one type or another were sorted out and handled separately.

I checked the receipts and the recordings and the tare weight on the truck against the petty cash receipts. Payment was entirely handled through a so-called petty cash operation. What a misnomer! The petty cash expended over the course of a year was in excess of $800,000. Nevertheless, everything seemed in order. The tallies were correct; I had made some tests of trucks coming in on a sample basis with my own staff that tallied with what was paid out of the petty cash, and so on.

The receipts were all properly annotated and nothing seemed remiss, except one clue. The petty cash fund was too small. Even though there was over $4,000 in the box when I counted the petty cash, it occurred to me that with this kind of operation, the cash on hand was inadequate to sustain each day's operations.

The truckers who came in with the big loads of steel would not come back if they were ever once not paid on the spot in cash. I will not go into the income tax ramifications of this; I think they are self-evident. Nevertheless, this was a big cash operation. And the petty cash fund, as I thought about it that night at the hotel, was just too small.

The business, though essentially a big corporate affair, was run by three brothers and two brothers-in-law, who were the plant chiefs and the corporate heads. As one of his major duties, one of the brothers-in-law operated this entire scrap steel operation. When I asked him about the size of the fund, his immediate reaction was, tell me how much you are short and I will write you a check for the difference!

I had found a clue that did not and should not have fit—the size of the fund. It seemed it was being used for a kind of personal replenishment—when the man in charge needed money for his own family or his own particular needs, he just helped himself. Later on, at the end of the month the difference was replaced, as I confirmed by checking other records in the cash journal. The brother-in-law would always make some kind of general restitution, calling it replenishment of the scrap steel cash fund.

The practice was very haphazard and, I think not intended in the long run to defraud the company, it was merely a poorly managed family aspect of this business, not fully understood by all the corporate family members, but at least condoned. On the other hand, when I told them about the check and the size of the cash fund, and we all discussed it, they said this type of sloppiness had to stop and that they would institute a better procedure.

The clue that didn't fit was the paucity of the petty cash, which seemed normal at first glance but which didn't fit the size of the operation.

CASE NO. 4. The next case involves a department store. One department seemed to be doing better than any other department in the entire store. The clue didn't fit.

The store had a steady clientele over the years and a rising business proportionately, increasing in each of the departments about the same each year, except for this one department, which was moving forward sharply in the last year.

I asked some of the executive sales managers why this was so, and as far as they could figure out, they attributed it to the aggressive sales technique of the manager there, and they were pleased by it. I thought to myself, how aggressive can you be? The whole store had a clientele that was very stable, and with a steady yearly increase, why would one department zoom out ahead of all the others? Customers aren't that easily impressed nowadays. The clue didn't fit.

I checked the inventories—physical inventories were taken monthly. It seemed their technique was reliable and on-line. The answer to the mystery was, of course, mark downs—very plentiful to stimulate sales but not transmitted to the accounting department.

SOME FURTHER THOUGHTS

Let me discuss what I consider to be the most important and far-reaching conceptual aspect of "The clues must fit" theory relating to modern-day accounting and the audits of the records accountants produce. I am referring, of course, to the balance sheet, which auditors endeavor to Certify (with a capital *C*) under a rigid and prescribed set of standards.

What does the balance sheet really say, in essence. They say in the vernacular of accounting shorthand that business *xyz* is worth a given amount of money. It has assets like cash, accounts receivable, inventories, land, fixed expenses, and so on that total a certain amount. It also has liabilities—accounts payable, long-term debts (such as mortgages), unpaid taxes, residual obligations to its employees (like future pension payouts, etc.). The net sum and substance of all this is the so-called equity of the business. It could be the property of only one person or corporation or it could be owned in varying portions by thousands (or even millions) of different stockholders.

The equity is the stated equity or *value* of the business—per the books—the familiar book value. But do all the clues fit? Is not the *true economic value* of anything in our democratic system essentially what it will bring in the free and open marketplace? But as we all know, the "book value" of any business, certified by any firm of auditors, is rarely the true value or going price of the business. Why? Because so many of the assets or liabilities never get recorded on the books, or are established in an artificial manner set in motion by rigid rules that are not very practical.

For instance, consider inventories. Their book value is what they cost—recorded in any consistent way—first in, first out; last in, last out; first in last out; big boxes first, sealed containers last; and so forth. It almost sounds like a children's game. But it is not.

Accountants and tax experts are dead serious about the process. But is the merchandise in the total inventory (book assets) salable? Maybe, for example, because the business has changed its main manufacturing line, much of its raw stock in the warehouse is now practically worthless to it. Is the stock the wrong color or fabric, or hardness of steel, or thickness of wood for the current, practical, day-to-day needs of this manufacturer or wholesaler?

If plant and equipment are modern enough to be economically useful for a legitimate business purpose, then a firm's net worth may be close to its original recorded value, less depreciation and scrap value. But if they are hopelessly outdated and cannot fit in with current needs, the true value is obviously much different. Need we look any further than some of our steel plants?

Let us consider some very important assets and liabilities that never get recorded on the books at all: personnel. Are the senior and key employees experienced, capable, satisfied with local living conditions (i.e., they are not tempted to change jobs or switch home sites)?

A store or service-related business has business potential. What is happening in the community? Will new highways favor competitors or force customers to bypass the business? Are nearby large plants opening or closing that will drastically change the economic "mix" of this area? Are new competitive products being introduced, or is a foreign corporation producing your main item at half the price or half the size, or twice as good (and getting government subsidies that will put you out of business)?

All these examples, and so many more, really dictate (and demonstrate) the correct value of a business much more than does a "Certified" balance sheet, in most cases. Ask any experienced businessman why he examines these unrecorded clues very carefully when buying or selling any business.

As auditors, you should expect to be called on to understand all of a firm's unrecorded assets and liabilities and estimate real net worth. This process is very much harder than the classic approaches to familiar balance sheet checking described in so many of our professional standards and texts.

So you must know how to make all the clues fit and be alert to any disparities or aberrations that stem from any quarter. This is what true, honest auditing is all about.

POINT SHEET

Why Do *All* the Clues Have to Fit?	The deviation from a norm may be important in itself It may show up a major weakness in controls. Systems that really work should not, logically, have big errors, even if small in number. Errors don't just melt away.
There Are Some Very Broad Aspects to the Overall Theme. Some Major Clues Are Elusive.	Balance sheets and profit and loss statements may be technically correct but artifically true. The true value of most business (especially smaller ones) should also consider nonbookkeeping assets and liabilities: personnel, sales potential, customer tastes, competitor inventions in the wings.

7

Mental Auditing, or What Could Go Wrong?

In the past, many auditors have insufficiently considered the importance of the detection of fraud (or abuse, or gross inefficiency) as a prime audit objective. But more and more pressure in recent years has been brought by all segments of the public—even the most sophisticated users of financial statements—for auditors to expand their roles and actively think about what could go wrong—and to find it!

THE APPROACH

The logical process in response to this is to put yourself in the mental shoes of a potential perpetrator and see if you can beat the system. The ways of doing this are extremely diverse and vary enormously with every different business operation. It would be fruitless to do more in this chapter than to cite a number of almost random selections to merely whet the interest (and lighten the concern) of the reader.

WORRISOME POSSIBILITIES

Be alert, for instance, when reviewing a corporation to see that the chief officers are not abusing their executive privileges or taking unfair advantage of their status. This point is in sharp and direct response to one of the main tenets of the AICPA Standards: Management represents a greater risk to auditors than do all the lower levels of operational supervision. It is higher-level executives who do (or do not) establish true separation of functions, which is more important than accounting controls (if you had to choose between them). Top management can overrule or subvert operations. It is top management that chooses key personnel and sets levels of competence, integrity, and independence.

In a single ownership or closely held business, the principle danger is usually the so-called trusted employee who is frequently handling the whole or a discrete and separate part of the operation, completely under his or her own authority. Cash businesses are, of course, particularly vulnerable. The auditor must constantly be alert as to where the receipts are held (physically), where they are coming from, and how payments are made. Any business, such as a restaurant, scrap metal or paper recovery business, where daily cash receipts are also used for payment of new material, is added cause for concern. A really good auditor, however, will in all cases be sharply aware of what's going on in and about the entire business. He (or she) will listen (audit) to the people for any aberrations of personality. He will watch the flow of people, goods, and paperwork as he goes about his full examination. He will also think through what a good norm would be *before* he examines the books and documents. There are any number of ways that a business can be ripped off, and the auditor will probably never be in a position to find most of them unless he takes the attitude that he can and should see into many of these things in advance. Let me illustrate all of these points by a limited number of examples just to demonstrate some aspects of this concept.

Example 1. The auditor is checking insurance charges in any business. What should be the first set of questions he ought to ask himself? Who is the broker? Who does the client make payments to—directly to the insurance company or straight to the independent insurance agent? If it is the independent insurance agent, the first thing to check is whether the parent insurance company has published its charges and rates. Also very important, what rebates have been issued in the last year? If there were any, double check to see that the insurance broker has passed them on to the client. If not, recommend a new broker and a full review of past transactions.

Example 2. In the restaurant business, there are hundreds of thousands of restaurants, diners, clubs, bars and grills, hotels of every size, family eating places, and fast-food outlets all over the country. It's probably the single most widespread business entity in many countries. It would take an entire book to point out the opportunities that exist for abuse in the restaurant business. There could hardly be an independent auditor in the Western world who doesn't at one time or another have a client with some relationship to the food industry or liquor sales. What is there to look for? If the auditor puts his mind to it, and he should, he should be able to mentally visualize thousands (literally) of ways that his client can get ripped off (a somewhat vulgar expression, but apt in this business). Let's take incoming merchandise—meat, fowl, fish, for instance. Is there a scale? Is it in use? Are the weights on the noncommercial packages accurate? Who weighs it in? Is the food coming in frozen or defrosted? Has the meat been pumped full of water (not at all hard to do). Who takes out the trash, or garbage? In what form does he or she take it out—bags, barrels, and so forth? Is the food storage area near a trash room that can easily be filled with roasts, chops, expensive liquors, and so on. This is easily one of the most vulnerable aspects of the whole restaurant food business. Sales slips are important. Waiters and waitresses have been known to cheat management by deliberately undercharging the amount of bill, hoping for bigger tips from their steady customers (who recognize that they are constantly being undercharged). What about bar charges? There are thousands of ways of being taken—glass sizes, watering down the liquor, changing the content of the bottles, substitutions, ringing up the wrong amounts on the cash register (hoping for bigger tips), and so on. In many areas of the country it is standard for bar owners to automatically fire bartenders after two months of less-than-expected gross profits compared to previously recorded norms. Many bar owners will even employ undercover people to watch the operation from time to time. They will take chemical readings of the liquor to see if it is being watered down.

The abusive possibilities of small or large retail stores are also mind-boggling. Customer shoplifting is a huge subject in itself. Chapter 9 covers computerized records.

As for assets that can be stolen, the main concern is whether they are portable. Big pieces are less vulnerable. The reader should "think like a thief" and then make appropriate tests to try and mentally catch himself.

Let me offer just one more situation to illustrate the overall point. Lottery tickets are springing up in many cities and states around the country in an effort to painlessly ease budget crunches. One popular sales method involves instant scratch cards. The buyer pays a dollar or two and gets a cardboard ticket with metallic coatings on it. By rubbing the coating off with a coin or fingernail you can see what's inscribed or imprinted underneath and learn whether you're a winner or not, instantly. They are very appealing to itinerant gamblers. These cards are usually sold all over—newspaper stands, drug stores, liquor stores, and so on. They are handled by thousands of unrelated small-business people. How should a perceptive auditor think about them?

It looks like a good system, prenumbered and all accounted for in advance. Well, if I were a city or state auditor, I would wonder whether you could run these cards past a laser beam, x-ray, or ultraviolet scanner or something similar and somehow determine what was imprinted underneath. The big winners could be withheld from regular sales by the dealers and kept for their own friends or relatives with little danger of exposure. In this fantastic era of superelectronic scanning devices, would this be so hard to do?

The point to this improvised mental picture of a possible abusive action is that good auditors should do this exercise all the time, everywhere they turn. It is not an idle game. Good practice prescribes it.

POINT SHEET

What Could Go Wrong	Spotting fraud and abuse grows more burdensome all the time. The way to do this is to put yourself in the mind of a would-be abuser, how could you do it, if so minded? Could it be done systematically or can one-shot abuses (even large ones) take place without detection? Be especially careful about top-management subversion of working internal controls.

PART FOUR

Verification: Extending the Survey Results

The first and most important question auditors must ask themselves when they gather evidentiary material is *why* are they checking out that particular evidence. Too many auditors routinely verify practically everything, by sampling or other means. This attitude stems from insecurity, the survey phase should have told the auditor what was strong or of little risk and needed no further verification.

Areas that appeared to be "squishy" could be tested further with a set of regular techniques—interviews, confirmations, comparisons, running down valid samples of documentation in great detail, using computer matching processes for material aberrances, and so forth. The material in this part is designed

---

Note to the reader: Let me suggest that you study the Point Sheet on this section before proceeding with this text. It should help to clarify how the various parts of this important subject fit together.

to help the auditor through the verification mill by understanding how and when to check things out expeditiously and reliably.

8

Sampling for Modern Auditing: Underlying Logic and Practical Techniques

BEFORE TAKING ANY SAMPLE

Every auditor must ask himself (or herself) *before* he takes a sample—any sample—what am I testing and why am I testing it? And—this is a very big question—what will I do with the results? How will I characterize them, and how will this assessment fit into the overall examination?

All too often, during the course of their review, auditors will sample transactions, perform their tests, and then try to figure out what to do with the results. This is all wrong! Thinking should come first. The mechanical part, or sampling, should follow. Sampling is, and should be, a *mechanical* process, much like using an adding machine, a calculator, or a computer.

Having put sampling in its proper place, let me describe the best way to proceed. Consider again the basic phases of an audit (preliminary, survey, verification, summary, and reporting). Generally, with minor exceptions, sampling is most useful in the survey and verification phases. Samples must be particularly responsive to each separate audit objective at each point of the review. Again, samples must be tailor-made to do each special audit job. Before explaining this, let me repeat an important thought: Good auditing always involves a pattern of effort with a necessary *rhythm* to it. One good logical step should follow each building block before it. Furthermore, if the whole requires careful construction, then it follows that each of the parts must have a step-by-step orderliness or the whole will not be the sum of its parts. The total effort will be disjointed. The resultant audit report will surely reflect such imbalances. Good supervisory and experienced reviewers can smell weaknesses in the audit performance, without ever looking at any detailed workpapers, just by reading wobbly narrations.

The rhythmic process involving the mechanics of sampling itself can be characterized as a simple three-step operation.

GOOD SAMPLING TECHNIQUES

Before doing anything else, the auditor must clearly understand the fundamental difference between the two (and there are only two) broad classes of samples. A sample is either a "probability" sample or a "judgment" sample. The probability or true random sample cannot be considered to be scientifically sound unless it meets the fundamental test of scientific experimentation. That is, following the law of probability, there must be a known chance of selection on each draw of a sampling unit from the population of all sampling units. This, in turn, sets the stage for replicating the sampling results, from the same field, for successive samples, all the time.

It's not hard to understand why this is true. Let's consider one small area of sampling–discovery sampling. We can predict what will happen if we know a single fact x and we use probability sampling to find an example of fact x. This sentence sounds somewhat soupy, but stay with me.

For example, let's assume we are looking at a population of 25 million vouchers. Furthermore, 500 of the vouchers contain errors, a fact that we are calling x. Now, suppose you tell me you want to find at least one erroneous voucher and that you propose to find it in a random sample of 100. I can confidently predict that there is a 0.2 percent chance that you will succeed in your objective. On your second try, with another sample of 100, there is still a 0.2 percent chance of success. Thus, we have the same chances of success in successive samples.

Let's turn the example around. Suppose you don't know how many erroneous vouchers there are in the total of 25 million. That is usually the case with auditors. "After all," the auditor can reasonably say, "if I know the rate of error I would not need to take a sample." Fair enough. But since the rules of probability remain constant, we can just change our hypothesis, and say something like this: "If the population does contain 500 errors, and if I sample 100, what is the probability that I will find at least one voucher that has an error?" The answer stays the same as before–0.002, or 0.2 percent. To show you how far this can be carried, see Table 1, which lists the chances of finding at least one voucher with an error, assuming a population size of 25 million, with differing sample sizes and different rates of error. If you study the table, I'm sure you will easily see how discovery (probability) sampling can be used to predict what will happen. Remember, our assumed population size is 25,000,000. The body of Table 1 contains the probabilities that a sample of a given size will contain at least one occurrence of the error being sought–assuming that the entire population has the number of occurrences shown in the column heads.

MORE ON PROBABILITY SAMPLING (THE REAL WORKHORSE)

The highest form of sampling–the one that requires the most stringent precision in the entire business world–is used when legal and financial settlements hinge on the results. In such cases,

Table 1. Relationship of Probability Sampling to Discovery Sampling

If the sample size is	[500] .002000%	[1,000] .004000%	[2,000] .008000%	[10,000] .040000%	[50,000] .200000%	[250,000] 1.000000%	: Occurrence : Probability
	(%)	(%)	(%)	(%)	(%)	(%)	
100	.2	.4	.8	3.9	18.1	63.4	
or 500	2.1	2.3	5.1	18.6	63.4	99.3	
or 1,000	2.1	2.3	10.3	31.9	86.3	99.9+	
or 5,000	29.1	56.6	79.1	94.1	99.9+	99.9+	
or 7,000	39.9	63.2	82.3	95.0	99.9+	99.9+	
or 10,000 (etc.)	39.8	63.2	82.3	95.0	99.9+	99.9+	

my basic "Rule of 200" takes hold. I believe that no less than 200 items, selected at random in a homogeneous universe, are acceptable to appeals boards or civil courts when contested results are at stake. Recent mathematical studies have borne out this rule of thumb, conceptually. It has also been checked by current computer analyses of 100 percent of all the items in a given verification, testing a given, previously sampled universe.

This is not to say—and this is very important—that the minimum 200-item sample will withstand legal challenge. On the other hand, while unrestricted samples of fewer than 200 are less precise, they are equally scientific in that successive samples of, say, 30 or 50 will result in a similar error percentage. Also, they will be equally probable in being wrong up to a measurable point. Therefore:

1. *Any* probability sample is absolutely valid (if drawn correctly from a homogeneous universe) in a predictable range of correctness, at a given confidence level.
2. Samples of 200 or more, when drawn correctly, are very much more precise, and dollar settlements based on them can be confidently sustained anywhere.
3. The scientific prerequisites of sample accuracy in a sample of any size are a good universe, random selection, and

precise terms as to what is to be considered in each situation or document—what is right and wrong according to agreed-on definitions established *before* the sample is drawn. This sampled performance (which must be replicable) and precise reporting, with no overreaching, should be the end product.

JUDGMENTAL SAMPLING—USEFUL IN ITS PLACE

So much for probability sampling. Judgmental sampling is vastly more subtle, less scientific, and consequently harder to use correctly or understand precisely. But it is an effective tool of the working auditor as basic as the tools that hang on a mechanic's belt.

Take an extreme situation, first, just to dramatize the point. Could the reader visualize a situation in which a sample of 1, drawn at random, would be conclusive? Let me construct several such situations to get the reader to think about this vital aspect of auditing.

The auditor has a client who has a quirk about color—he insists every piece of stationery used in his business be soft cream-colored because, he maintains, it creates a positive feeling among his customers. The auditor establishes in his survey that only one printer supplies the paper and also that only one large order was placed. Receiving records showed only one delivery to date in a single large, sealed box. Would it not follow that the auditor could reach in, select one single sheet, and if it were soft cream-colored, be assured that the client's wishes had been carried out?

I'm sure that the reader, following this line of thought, can picture circumstances in which this would not hold true. But this is not the point. The point is, a sample of 1 *can* be conclusive in the right circumstances. If one wishes another example, take the case of having to decide what the magnetic field of a sealed box is; every particle, or group of particles, will register positive or negative on sufficiently sensitive recorders. One sample should suffice, shouldn't it?

Could an auditor prove a valid hypothesis to be absolutely correct just by fishing around? Of course! The auditor has observed that a firm employs sloppy receiving and check-in methods and feels that some bills may have been paid twice as a result. The office manager disagrees. To prove the point, the auditor can scan many of the purchase orders, fixing dollar amounts in his mind. Then he can "run through" the cash disbursements journal: Any payment appearing twice is instantly suspect and can quickly prove the point. It will not, however, tell him how many errors there are, but only that they might exist at all. The extent of the inaccuracies could be ascertained only by the use of a probability sample. How precisely the auditor needs to know the amount of error would dictate the size of the sample.

Suppose the auditor to prove a fraud case needs only one bona fide instance of a shipment sent to a fraudulent firm, Company ABC. Obviously, any way he finds the incriminating document will suffice. Perhaps the easiest is to ask the office clerks if they remember any document pertaining to Company ABC in the files. They might walk over and pick it right out for you.

Therefore, it is safe to say that judgment samples have many uses and are, in their own way, another useful methodology for auditors, much like physical observations, interviewing personnel, or making studies of like industries or similar businesses. But judgment samples cannot stand on their own like a true probability sample, scientifically drawn from a "clean" field.

The primary disadvantage of a nonprobability sample is that it cannot readily be defended as being representative of the data from which it was drawn. For example, compare the representativeness of the auditor's selecting, say, every tenth paid voucher for review with a method in which item selection is based solely on the auditor's judgment. The notion that a certain percentage of the total number of items must be included in a sample finds no support in either logic or in sound sampling practice. On the contrary, it often leads to oversampling and, frequently, unsound conclusions.

Many books have been written on one or another of the various aspects of sampling. The reader can consult them for learning close-in, often esoteric techniques such as estimation sampling, acceptance sampling, exploratory sampling, random numbers, stratified sampling, cluster sampling, multistate sampling, and standard deviation. Few texts, however, fully explain the underlying theory in lay terms. Therefore, I am going to further illustrate in relatively simple terms the essence of probabilities and averages and their applications. A few formulas (the fewest possible) that should be mastered are included as a part of this discussion.

Let us now again reconsider some salient points. Auditors face the task of reviewing large masses of data to arrive at audit conclusions. That is a fact of our professional life from which there is no escape. And because of the computer, data volume seems to be growing larger than ever. It is not uncommon for auditors to be charged with reviewing files that contain hundreds of thousands, or even millions, of transactions.

When faced with such situations, "sampling" is an attractive (maybe the only) alternative to large-scale examinaton. There are two classes of samples: (1) probability samples, and (2) judgment (nonprobability) samples.

BACK TO PROBABILITY SAMPLING

A probability sample can be defended as being representative (within specified limits) of the data from which it was drawn. And, we can apply criteria to guide us in limiting our sample to the minimum size necessary.

A very useful and informative way of studying probability sampling is to review these related concepts:

Averages—their meaning and uses.

Measures of dispersion—what they are and why they are important.

The normal distribution—what it is and its relationship to probability sampling.

Probability distributions—what they are, what they portray, and their tie-in to sampling odds.

Grasping the underlying reasoning that supports these four general concepts helps auditors to function well, with minimal difficulty, in applying probability sampling during almost any audit. Probability sampling draws heavily upon each of the concepts for its support.

One should also find it useful to have handy a definition of three terms that will be used frequently during this discussion.

Population. A population consists of the *entire* field from which a sample is drawn. For example, if you are assigned to review paid travel claims for a certain finite period, the population consists of *all* travel claims that were paid during the audit period. A population is also sometimes referred to as the *universe.*

Sampling unit. A population consists of a number of sampling units. In the population of paid travel claims, each paid travel claim is a sampling unit.

Sample. A sample consists of two or more sampling units that are selected from all sampling units in the entire population.

A Word of Caution

The purpose of a sample is to permit the auditor to develop a summary value that is representative of the population's actual summary, or total, value. An example might be the "average" hourly wage paid to all employees. But we should be very careful in the use of the term *average.* There are many different types of averages. All can be computed from the same data. You should always be familiar with the characteristics of any average that you use. Here are three principal ones:

Measures of Central Tendency

Arithmetic Mean

The arithmetic mean is commonly referred to as the average. It is widely used and easy to compute. Calculate it by (1) summing the values in a sample or population, and (2) dividing the summed total by the number of values included in the total. One important problem with the arithmetic mean is that it is "pulled" in the direction of extreme values. We said earlier that the purpose of a sample is to develop a summary value that is representative of the population's summary value. Let's establish a hypothetical population and observe the effect on the population's mean if we include a value far above other values. Then, perhaps, it will not be difficult to visualize the effect of extreme values that may be present in a sample. Assume that we have a population composed of the positive values 5, 5, 10, 15, 20, 25, 30, 35, and 4355. The population's actual summary value (mean) is +500. Notice that the mean is strongly influenced (one could say biased) by the value 4355. Do you believe that the +500 is typical of values in the population? However, it is discretely representative of the field if there are no extremes. One illustrative and practical aspect of knowing, instinctively, the mechanics and nuances of averages can be shown in this fashion. Suppose, for example, you are surveying the operations of a large multistoried furniture showroom that has all kinds of items—chairs, desks, lamps, mirrors, couches, tables, rugs, objects d'art, bedroom sets, even whole kitchens complete with counters and appliances. You would have made notes about the recorded book value of this entire inventory previously. The items in backup, crated or packaged in storage are easier to add up and mentally absorb. But one could, with practice, get a pretty good feel for the sum of the values of the floor items by mental averaging, that is, by estimating the "mean average" of the sum and multiplying by the number of items you see. This could work in a large store with a coordinated range of items, not heavily or abnormally skewed by a lot of small or very large pieces.

So, if the books reflect a $2,500,000 total and your instinctive (and practiced) estimate is only $1,500,000, it's a good time to look a little deeper into the situation than you would normally do.

Averaging can, of course, be used in many ways, limited only by the auditor's ingenuity.

Median

The median of a sample or population is the middle value if the number of sampling units is odd, or the arithmetic mean of the two middle values if the number of sampling units is even. Consider again our population values 5, 5, 10, 15, 20, 25, 30, 35, and 4355. The median is the middle value, or 20. Do you believe that the median for our example is more typical of the population values than is the +500 arithmetic mean? Of course it is (in this case).

Mode

The mode is the "most prevalent" value or thing. In our example, the mode is 5. Do you believe that the mode is more typical of the population values than either the arithmetic mean (+500) or the median (20)? You might ask, Under what circumstances should I use any of the three averages? The answer depends on many factors, most of which are outside the scope of sampling. But different averages are desirable for differing purposes. Do you desire a composite average of all items in the population, as is used in sampling? If your answer is yes, use the arithmetic mean. Do you desire the middle value? If so, use the median. Or, perhaps you are seeking the most frequent value. Then, use the mode. The concept to be remembered at this point is that the arithmetic mean may or may not be typical of values in the population. The mean, alone, does not give us any indication of how typical it may be.

On the basis of our knowledge of each sampling unit in the population, we concluded that the +500 mean in our example was not typical of individual values in the population. But frequently, such information is not available. When this is the case, there is a method we can use to judge how close an arithmetic mean that we compute from a probability sample might be to the actual mean of the population. This method is what makes probability sampling such a powerful management tool. To illustrate the point, let us assume the 9 values in our previous example (i.e., 5, 5, 10, 15, 20, 25, 30, 35, and 4355) represent the values included in a *sample* from a population that contains 1,000 sampling units. (We will learn later that a sample size should, at a minimum, exceed 30. We will use a sample size of 9 in this case merely to illustrate a statistical relationship. We could have used, say, 35 values. But the illustration would become cumbersome.) As is done in sampling, we will use the mean of the 9 values (the sample mean, which is +500) as an estimate of the actual mean of the population. We hope that the +500 is typical of the population's mean. But how typical? Let us assume we use the +500 mean and each of the 9 values to make a few simple computations. The results allow us to add two other very important ingredients by stating that (1) The actual mean of the population is somewhere between −606.76 and +1606.76 and that (2) We have a 95 percent chance of being correct.

We can all agree that the two additional ingredients add significantly to the quality of our estimating procedure. They provide an insight into the reliability of the +500 estimate. In our example, the actual mean could take on a wide range of values. Now, would you conclude that the +500 arithmetic mean computed from our sample is typical of the population's actual mean? Here is another example. Assume that we select a sample of 8 units from a population containing 1000 units. The arithmetic mean computed from our sample equals +18.13. We make some additional computations and find that we have a 95 percent chance of being correct if we state that the actual mean value in the population is somewhere between +8.93 and +27.33. Do you believe that the +18.13 mean computed from our second sample is more reliable than the +500 mean computed from our first sample? We will study this concept more as our discussion proceeds. But for now, let us make this observation: In our first example there was a significant difference between the arithmetic mean (+500) of our sample and the limits we assigned to the population's mean (−606.76) to +1606.76). In the second example, the limits (+8.93 to +27.33) when compared to the sample's mean (+18.13) were not as great. *Dispersion*, or variability as it is sometimes called, has a significant influence on how wide the limits will be. And dispersion is our next topic.

Measures of Dispersion

Dispersion is the variation in data and is as important as the arithmetic mean itself. Consider again the +500 mean that we computed during our study of averages. The dispersion in the values—particularly the one value of 4355—had a significant influence on our results. If we eliminate the 4355 and consider only the remaining eight values, the mean becomes +18.13. So, we can see that dispersion in our example caused the mean to vary widely. The variation can be so great, in fact, that we need to measure it in order to assess the reliability of the averages (means) we compute.

The most widely used measure of dispersion in probability sampling is called the *standard deviation*. There are other measures, such as the *range*—the difference between the largest and smallest values. In our 9 values (5, 5, 10, 15, 20, 25, 30, 35, and 4355) the range is 4350, or 4355 less 5. A disadvantage of the range is that it does not give us any information about the dispersion of intervening values—only the largest and the smallest. For that reason, it is seldom used.

The standard deviation overcomes objections to the range. It measures dispersion of all units being studied and is the standard measure of dispersion in probability sampling. So that you can more easily grasp the concept of the standard deviation, let's establish a hypothetical population consisting of the values 5, 5, 10, and 10. The standard deviation measures dispersion from the arithmetic mean. The mean equals 7.50. Now, compare the 7.50

with each of the four values in the population and answer this question, "On the average and expressed in the same units as the mean, how far does each item in the population vary from the mean?" If your answer is 2.50 you are correct, and you have computed the standard deviation of our hypothetical population. So, you see, there is nothing complicated about the standard deviation. It only becomes cumbersome to compute when each value does not vary from the mean by the same amount. Consider the values 4, 5, 14, 20, and 37. The mean equals 16. Using the same method as before, compute the standard deviation. You can't? You could, very easily, if you were given a list of procedures to follow in computing the standard deviation for any population. Here they are:

1. Allow for three columns on a workpad.
2. In column 1, enter each population value.
3. In column 2, enter the difference between the mean and each population value. For example, if the mean is 16 and the population value is 37, the difference is 21.
4. In column 3, enter the square of each difference in column 2. If the difference is 21, the square is 441.
5. Sum column 3 and divide the total by the number of units in the population.
6. Obtain the square root of the result. The answer is the standard deviation.

Note: The discussion that follows has some math in it that you may have studied years ago and promptly forgot. More explicitly, it calls for finding the square root of a number—any number. So, if you have forgotten how to find a square root of a number—and really could care less—let me give you a way to arrive at the answer without having to once again wend your way through mathematical formulas and algebraic briar patches.

If, for example, you want the square root of 12, start with as close a guess as you can, off the cuff, and square the number (squaring is easy) to see how close it comes to 12. In this case try 3. Now 3 times 3 equals 9—not close enough. Next try 4; but 4 times 4 equals 16, further away. Therefore, since 3 squared is 9, which is 3 less than 12, and 4 squared is 16, or 4 more than 12, the right number must be about half way between 3 and 4, or about 3.6. Multiply 3.6 times 3.6 and you get 12.96—too much. Next try 3.5. This multiplies out to 12.25—getting close. Try 3.49. This results in 12.18. The pattern is clear and 3.47 should do it. Getting there; 3.47 times 3.47 is 12.0409, very close. Try 3.469 times 3.469. Not yet—this comes to 12.0339. The next "guess" will do it—the square root of 12 should be 3.464 (accurate to the nearest 1/100th). Close enough! Eureka! You've taken the square root of 12 (proof—3.464 times 3.464 equals 11.999296). How close do you want to get?

Here is a formula for computing the standard deviation.

$$\delta = \sqrt{\frac{\Sigma(X - \overline{X})^2}{N}}$$

Where:

δ = standard deviation of population
$\sqrt{\ }$ = extract the square root of
Σ = sum the values
X = each population value
$\overline{X}$ = arithmetic mean (average) of population
N = total number of units in population

Note that we are talking about the standard deviation of a *population*. Later, we will discuss the procedure for estimating the standard deviation of a population from a *sample*.

One very important fact contains the clue to unraveling the so-called mystery of probability sampling.

> If you are dealing with *any* large population whose values, or other characteristic being measured, are distributed within the population so that they form a normal distribution (represented by a symmetrical, bell-shaped curve, which we will discuss shortly, you will invariably find that (if you made a 100 percent review of the population):

68 percent of the values in the population will be within one standard deviation of the mean.

90 percent of the values in the population will be within 1.65 standard deviations of the mean.

95 percent of the values in the population will be within 1.96 standard deviations of the mean.

99 percent of the values in the population will be within 2.58 standard deviations of the mean.

There are other factors. We have identified four. Let us apply two of them so you can more easily understand how the process works.

Normal Distribution

Assume that you are analyzing a population that is normally distributed. If you were to plot it, you would find that the graph looks like the cross section of a bell. This type of distribution is often called a *bell-shaped curve.* Technically, it is a normal distribution. Assume that the population's mean equals $100, with a standard deviation of $10. Based upon this information, together with our knowledge that the population is normally distributed, we can conclude that 68 percent of all values in the population are within $10 of the mean—or between $90 and $110. Likewise, 95 percent of the values are within $19.60 ($10 times 1.96) of the mean, or between $80.40 and $119.60.

For some reason, a great amount of mystery seems to surround the normal distribution, perhaps because its properties just appear too simple. True, the mathematical formula that describes it is somewhat complex. But our purpose is not to gather an inventory of formulas. Even if you know nothing about advanced mathematics, you can still learn enough to make good and practical on-the-job use of the normal distribution.

We have already touched upon a most important property of normal distributions. If you know that a population is normally distributed and have computed its mean and standard deviation, then you can apply a factor to the standard deviation to determine the percentage of items that are within a specified distance from the mean. The working principle that you should not forget is this: Knowledge that a distribution is normal permits you to draw valid inferences. Later, we can use this same property to draw valid inferences about a mean we compute from a sample, even if the population from which the sample is drawn is not normally distributed. But for now, merely remember this most important property of a normal distribution.

Probability Distributions

A probability distribution is nothing more than a listing of all possible outcomes of a sample or other experiment and the probability of the occurrence of each outcome. So, if you desire to construct a probability distribution, it is necessary to:

Decide on the sample or experiment you desire to conduct.

List all possible outcomes of the sample or experiment.

Assign a probability to each outcome, using the addition or multiplication rule, as appropriate.

Let's construct a probability distribution of four tosses of a fair coin. Heads is identified by H and tails by T. The possible outcomes are (in the order of tosses) H, H; H, T; T, H; and T, T. Assume that we are interested in the probability of tossing a tail. In this case we are seeking the probability of one event or the other (heads or tails) and one event automatically eliminates the other. Therefore, we will use the addition rule for mutually exclusive events. A table showing the probabilities of tossing a tail during each flip of the coin is shown below.

There are many classes of probability distributions. Let's discuss two: the *binomial* and the *normal* distributions. The binomial distribution is used to show probabilities when two condi-

Outcome of Two Tosses of a Coin

No. of Tails	No. of Events	Probability
0	1	1/4
1	2	1/2
2	1	1/4
Totals	4	1

tions are satisfied. They are: (1) Each item drawn into the sample can be classified into one, and only one, of two categories—right or wrong, heads or tails, and so on; and (2) each item drawn into the sample is independent of all other items drawn into the sample. Consider the process of flipping a coin, for example. The probability of heads on the second flip is not affected by the results of the first flip. That is, there is a 0.5 chance of a head for the first flip. It is also 0.5 for the second flip, regardless of whether a head or tail results from the first. The result of each toss is independent of the results of other tosses, and the probability of tossing a head or a tail does not change as the tosses continue. A significant difference in probabilities computed under the two methods occurs when the sample size is large in relation to the population. In other cases, the binomial, or other than geometric distributions show similar probabilities for the same events. And because the formulas for the binomial distribution are easier to work with, they are frequently used in lieu of those for the hypergeometric. However, you should consider consulting someone who has knowledge of the hypergeometric and binomial distributions if (1) your sample size is large in comparison to the population, and (2) you desire to project *attributes* from your sample. Properties of the distribution (binomial or hypergeometric) are used to set the lower and upper limits of your sample estimate. We will study the meaning of lower and upper limits later in our discussion. You may be puzzled regarding how to recognize when a "sample size is large in comparison to the population." The sample size may be large when it is 20 percent or more of the population. To give you an idea of differing probabilities computed from a large sample, consider the above table showing the probability of tossing two tails in succession. Using rules for the binomial distribution, the probability, computed for a hypergeometric distribution, is zero because there is no chance of two tails since the one and only tail would be removed from the population the first time it appeared. It is removed because the hypergeometric distribution does not assume an "infinite" population or sampling with replacement. As you can see, the difference is significant indeed. And, when you think about it, auditors do not usually select samples from an "infinite" population or follow sampling with replacement procedures. (Refer to the second of the conditions for the binomial distribution, above.)

Another interesting application of mathematical probability theory to auditing is seen in what mathematicians often refer to as the *birthday problems*. The question posed by the birthday problem is this: What is the probability that a fixed group (any size) of persons will have (or will not have) at least two people with the same month and day of birth? Mathematicians have found a handy formula for computing the answer. You can use the formula to help you make decisions during audits.

Before getting to the formula, let me explain how the birthday problem relates to our audit work. Suppose you are doing an audit of personnel records. You look at the first 10 folders in the file. You put those back and look at the next 10. You notice two people (with similar names) have the same month and day of birth. Thinking that to be odd, you go back and look at the first 10 again. you find the same thing–two people with the same birthday. Strange, you think. You look at the third group of 10 and find it again! Now your suspicion is really high, so you look at all groups of 10.

At the end, you find that over 50 percent of the groups of 10 personnel folders contain two people's records that show the same month and day of birth. Could this be a coincidence? Not very likely!

What do I mean by "not very likely?" When you look at the personnel records in groups of 10, there is a 12 percent (rounded off) chance that you will find at least two people, in any one group, with the same month and day of birth. Stated another way, about 12 percent of the groups of 10 can be expected to contain what you found—but not over 50 percent. Something other than pure chance caused such a high rate of occurrence. The clues don't fit! Now, the auditor (you) must find the cause: fictitious employees? a lot of twins? inaccurate birth date information? duplicate personnel files (and pay checks)?

So, we see that probability can play a role in the auditor's decision process. Let me explain how to compute the probabilities for yourself, in a one-two-three setup fashion. I will use my example of groups of 10 to illustrate. You can change the group size to whatever you wish.

1. First, multiply 365 × 364 × 363 × . . . × 356. The answer is 37 followed by 24 zeros, rounded off. (There are 365 days in each year. So, the first person has 365 possibilities. The second person has only 364, because we subtract 1 day on which there might be a match with the first person. And so on, back 10 times, because there are 10 people in the group.)
2. Second, multiply 365 by itself 10 times. The answer is 42 followed by 25 zeros, rounded off. (This is the total number of possible matches.)
3. Divide 37 by 42. The answer is .88, which is the probability that a birth date match *will not* be found in any one group of 10. To find the probability that it will happen, merely subtract .88 from 1, giving .12, or 12 percent.

The normal distribution is used to show probabilities when there are infinite outcomes to an experiment. Consider, for example, the case when our objective is to arrive at the average value of each inventory item. Each item varies in price, and our final estimate can take on an infinite number of values. Hence, the sampling units, as well as our final estimate, vary. They are not classified as right or wrong, over a limit or under a limit, heads or tails, and so on. So we rely on the normal distribution when we sample variables.

The usefulness of probability distributions may seem abstract to you. How can they benefit you during your audits? First of all, perhaps we should point out that it is not necessary for you to construct them during your work. You merely rely on their properties when you apply probability sampling.

Let's return to our earlier discussion of the normal distribution (the bell-shaped curve). If you remember, we stated that if we had knowledge of a normally distributed population's mean and standard deviation, we could determine the percentage of the population's units that were within specified limits. The concept of the normal distribution can even be applied to all possible sample means that could be drawn from a population. That's because if you were to compute and plot all possible means (pounds, dollars, time, etc.) that could be selected from a population and if your sample size is large enough (over 30 as a minimum), the distribution would be *normal.* And that concept applies almost regardless of the distributions of the population. Such a distribution is called the sampling distribution of the mean. It has a central place in probability sampling.

One example of the sampling distribution of the mean consists of listing all possible samples of two that can be drawn from a population of six. The population will not form a normal distribution. Yet, one will find that (1) the "sampling distribution of the mean" will approach the normal form; and (2) the most prevalent means within the sampling distribution of the mean will equal or nearly equal the population mean. These results will be used to build confidence that we can rely upon the properties of probability distributions during our audit work. If the sample size is sufficiently large and if we give each sampling unit in the population an equal chance of selection–and thereby each mean an equal chance–we are most likely to select a mean that equals or nearly equals, the population's actual mean. That's because (1) sample means cluster much more closely around the population mean than do the original values, and (2) the larger the sample, the closer the sample mean is likely to be to the mean of the entire population. If the most prevalent means are means that equal or nearly equal the actual mean, then the most prevalent means are most likely to be selected. Also, if the sampling distribution of the mean forms a normal curve, we can apply the properties of normal curves to determine the reliability of the mean we select during our audit.

The normal distribution becomes even more useful because the binomial distribution takes on the normal form as the sample size is increased or as the probability inherent in the population (error rate, for example) closely approximates 50 percent. So the normal distribution plays an important role in probability sampling.

We have been discussing quite a bit of the thinking that supports probability sampling. But we haven't discussed the probability sample itself and how to select and interpret one.

The Probability Sample

Selecting and interpreting a probability sample is quite simple and in fact, does not depend on your understanding of the previous topic. Properly applied, it will work for you, like your automobile does (most of the time) even though you may not be a mechanic. The only dangerous thing about such an approach is that you will not know how to "fix" your sample if anything goes wrong. Or you may fix the wrong thing. Or, it may not be working and you might not even know it.

I used an automobile mechanic in lieu of an automobile engineer in this illustration on purpose. It is entirely feasible for auditors to gain all of the logic necessary to fully apply probability sampling and not be statisticians. Nor do we need to be. The professional statistician has made a tool available to us. All we must do is to understand it and know how to use it.

Probability samples may take a variety of forms, appropriate for various situations.

Unrestricted random samples

Sampling for attributes
Sampling for variables

Stratified random samples
Sampling for attributes
Sampling for variables

Cluster samples

Multistage samples

Acceptance sampling

Discovery sampling

Interval sampling

Dollar-unit sampling

Selecting a probability sample

Defining the population

Selecting sampling units from the population
Tables of random numbers
Random numbers generated by the computer

What is the meaning of the results and how can we use them? In answering this question, recall the topics already discussed that provide the support for probability sampling. As an example to pull all of the topics together, assume that you have been assigned to determine whether the total recorded value of accounts receivable, as shown in ABC Company's records, is reasonably correct. You determine that there are 3000 open accounts with a recorded value of $165,000. Your analysis of the accounts shows that almost all have a balance that ranges between $25 and $75. None exceeds $100. You decide on an unrestricted random sample because variability in the population does not appear to warrant a stratified sample.

Using a table of random numbers, you select 35 of the accounts for review. You decided on 35 because you know that the sample size should, at a minimum, exceed 30 for you to be reasonably certain that the "sampling distribution of the mean" will form a normal curve.

You audit the 35 accounts and compute a mean value of \$41 and a standard error of the mean of \$10. Perhaps we should digress a bit and explain the term *standard error of the mean.* It is nothing more than the standard deviation of the sampling distribution of the mean. It is not called *standard deviation* to differentiate it from the standard deviation of the population. It is computed somewhat differently, as explained below.)

Compute the standard deviation from the sampling units in your sample. Refer to the procedure we have already discussed for computing a standard deviation. There is one modification you should make–divide by the sample size minus one. The result will be an estimate of the *population* standard deviation, computed from your sample. You should divide by the sample size minus one because population standard deviations estimated from samples tend to be understated. If we subtract one from the sample size, we compensate.

Divide the estimate of the population standard deviation by the square root of the sample size.

Multiply the result by the square root of the ratio of sampling units in the population that were not sampled, (computed by dividing the number of items in the population *not* included in the sample by the number of items in the population minus one). Of course, before taking the square root, the ratio should be expressed as a decimal. This is called the *finite correction factor.* We use it because the computed standard error of the mean tends to be overstated when a large percentage of the population's sampling units are included in a sample or when we sample from a small population.

Here is the formula:

$$\delta\bar{x} = \left(\frac{\delta}{\sqrt{n}}\right)\left(\sqrt{\frac{N-n}{N-1}}\right) \quad \text{Finite Correction Factor}$$

$\delta\bar{x}$ = Standard error of the mean

δ = Estimate of population standard deviation, computed from a sample

n = Number of units in sample

$\sqrt{\ }$ = The square root of

N = Number of units in the population

(Notice that the formula directs the same procedure as first outlined.)

Let's return to our example. The standard error of the mean is \$10. Based on our knowledge of the characteristics of the *normal distribution*, we can conclude that 68 percent of all means that could be selected from our population are within \$10 of the computed mean. Let's state this another way. The actual mean in the population is somewhere between \$31 and \$51, and we are 68 percent certain that we are correct. Based on our sample, our best estimate of the mean is \$41. So, the \$31 to \$51 is expressed at the 68 percent *confidence level.*

But the 68 percent confidence level is not sufficient for our purposes. We desire to be 95 percent certain of our results. So we merely multiply \$10 by a factor (see Table 1) of 1.96, giving us \$19.60. Now we can say that the actual mean is somewhere between \$21.40 and \$60.60, and we are 95 percent certain that we are correct. Still, our best estimate of the mean is \$41. The values used thus far are for one account. But there are 3000 accounts. No problem. Merely multiply each of the three values by 3000 to obtain estimates for the entire population. Thus, we can state that the actual value of accounts receivable is somewhere between \$64,200 and \$181,800 and that we are 95 percent certain we are correct. Based on our sample, our best estimate, of the value of accounts receivable is \$123,000.

If you decide that the range \$64,200 to \$181,800 is too great, you increase your sample, by using the table of random numbers, to, say, 300. After selecting 265 additional sampling units, for a total of 300, you find that the newly computed mean is \$44 and the standard error of the mean equals \$3. Again we multiply the standard error of the mean by 1.96 because we desire to be 95 percent confident of our results. Expressed for the average account in the population, we can state that the mean correct balance is somewhere between \$38.12 and \$49.88 and that we have a 95 percent chance of being correct. Our best estimate of the actual mean value is \$44. Expressed for the entire population, the actual total correct value of accounts receivable is somewhere between $114,360 and $169,640 and we have a 95 percent chance of being correct in making this estimate. Based on our sample, we conclude that the best estimate of the total value is $132,000.

Perhaps you noticed that our first sample mean ($41) differs from the mean of the second sample ($44). The difference between each of the means and the *actual* population mean is called the *sampling error.* I prefer another term, such as *sampling variation.* Regardless of the term we use, it refers to the difference between a mean computed from a sample and the actual population mean. Don't lose sight of the fact that the mean we select is only one of all possible means. Because different samples contain different elements of the population, their respective means will also differ.

You decide that the range expressed at the 95 percent confidence level ($114,360 to $149,640) is narrow enough. Based on your sample, you conclude that the $165,000 recorded value of accounts receivable is incorrect. But by how much? We would use our $132,000 as the estimate of the actual value. It is your *best point estimate* of the actual population mean, based on your sample of 300. But, assume that the ABC Company comptroller defends the $165,000 recorded value. In addition to the specific errors you may have found and that were disclosed by your sample, you have another powerful source of persuasion. There is a 95 percent chance that the actual value of accounts receivable is somewhere between $114,360 and $149,640. The conclusion is provable because you used probability sampling techniques. But it is also provable that there is a 5 percent chance that your $114,360 to $149,640 interval estimate is incorrect. If you have a 5 percent chance of being incorrect, there is a 2.5 percent chance that the actual value is less than $114,360 and a 2.5 percent chance that it is greater than $149,640, as the ABC Company comptroller maintains. But this means that you have a 97.5 percent chance that it is $149,640 or below. If you were top management, whom would you believe, the auditor or the comptroller?

Computer Matching

One aspect of sampling that is becoming more and more important is computer matching. It is not a sample, but rather a 100 percent comparison of a segment of a verification universe that happens to have its data computerized against another set of computer data (usually completed for different data purposes) to match like items for further audit verification. Most of the existing audit examples of this process have been developed and used by state and federal auditors who faced fields of data running into the hundreds of millions of data items and needed sophisticated mechanical help in sorting them out.

Computer matching is really the mechanical comparison of different lists or files to see if identical or similar items appear in both of them. For example, a list of persons with delinquent educational loans from sample school A can be taken and compared with a list of all federal employees to discover whether the same person appears on both lists.

Obviously a bona fide sample of both files (probability sample) can be drawn and compared and it can be then computed as to what the expected total number of "hits" (this term is defined shortly) are in the entire universe (with some caveats as to precision). This, however, only tells the auditor how many there probably are but does not identify *all* possible errors. How more potent the computer match can be than probability samples when all records to be compared are computer based!

Comparisons of this sort can involve names, social security numbers, addresses, contract numbers, numbers on bills or invoices, and much more. Such comparisons done by a computer are done quickly and relatively cheaply. The resulting list of identical or similar items, however, (and this must be clearly understood) must *then* be verified or investigated by a knowledgeable person. All that the computer establishes is that an apparently common item occurs in the information that was compared.

Why has the use of computer matching increased dramatically? There are two reasons. First, it is fast, efficient, and accurate. For a person to compare thousands of cases one by one by hand would be extremely tedious and time consuming. Considering the mountains of records that are piling up, it is becoming almost impossible to do this. High-speed computers, on the other hand, can process voluminous files quickly, comparing elements and records simultaneously that would otherwise require many separate manual operations. Since computers are not subject to human fatigue, results are far more accurate than manual processing.

Second, the results are a starting point for efforts to prevent and detect possible mistakes or even fraud. Similar or identical information can easily come to light as a result of matching efforts. The match provides a clue that can lead a manager to improve the efficiency of his or her operations, correct mistakes, cut down on waste, and uncover possible fraud.

What are some of the results to date of computer matching? There are many examples of computer matches where the results have been spectacular compared to the cost of doing the match. For example, the state of New York has been matching the records of welfare recipients with quarterly wage reports from New York employers. They estimate that they will save $95 million in 4 years from a system that cost $28 million—a return of almost 340 percent. The inspectors general of the Small Business Administration and the U.S. Department of Agriculture matched data on farm disaster loans from the Small Business Administration with data on Farmers Home Administration emergency loans made during the test year. Some 123 borrowers were found who had received over $2.3 million in duplicate loan benefits. Almost $1.3 million has been recovered. The match only cost $50,000. In California, computer matching has been used to find people who have been ordered by a court to repay overpayments from the Aid to Families with Dependent Children (AFDC) program since they had received state income tax refunds. The amount of such refunds, by regulation, should have reduced the recipient's payments from the program. These are just a few samples of the kind of results computer matching has produced in the past.

How is matching actually done? Comparing one list of information with another to discover duplications, gaps, and contradictions is an old analytical and investigative method. The application of computers to this traditional technique opens new possibilities by permitting quick and cheap comparisons of extremely large data bases, without the complications of dealing with separate lists and bulky records.

There are many types of computer matching, particularly in government programs in which payments are based on a recipient's demonstrated need. Many government agencies have pioneered in this work and their techniques are not private. In two of the largest programs–Food Stamps and Aid to Families with Dependent Children–federal legislation provides for matching. Applicants report information about income and assets; those whose total resources are below a certain amount are eligible for program participation. To cross-check their eligibility, lists of applicants and recipients are matched against quarterly wage and earning reports that employers file with the states for each employee to qualify them for the unemployment insurance program. If the same names appear on both rolls, the reported wages are checked to make sure that the total is under the cutoff amount for eligibility for food stamps or AFDC. Matches are often run not only against quarterly wage data but also against lists of recipients of other benefit programs, such as Social Security Old Age, Disability, and Supplemental Security Income and Railroad Retirement, to establish that total income from all resources does not exceed limits for AFDC or food stamp participation. Matches are also sometimes done against Medicaid and school enrollment records to check that the number of children a recipient claims to have (which determines the amount of benefits received) is accurate.

"Hit" Defined

What is a *hit*, and when is it important? A hit is information from two or more computer tapes that *appears* to be identical or similar. For example, the same name, social security number, address, or telephone number found during the computer tape comparisons would be a hit. At first it would be considered a raw hit–information that seems to match. Raw hits have to be audit verified. On investigation, they frequently prove to be duplications, coincidences, errors in recording names, or transpositions in numbers. If it is established that the information is really identical or similar, the hit is considered solid. Computer matching can do no more than this. Solid hits have to be checked further before it can be determined whether error or fraud exists.

What if data on the computer tape are wrong? Computers are no more accurate than the information stored in them. Names can be misspelled; digits in social security numbers can be transposed; birth dates can be inaccurately recorded. Mistakes like these can lead to erroneous matches or the apperance of impropriety. Fortunately, we know that decisions cannot be made on the basis of a computer match. All that a computer match can show is that the same or similar information appears in the files that were compared. Verification of the match and investigation into the case are necessary before any tentative conclusions can be drawn.

Another important factor in computer matching is deterrence. There is evidence that public knowledge of matching operations acts as a deterrent to fraud.

Shortly after the appearance of newspaper reports that state and federal officials were cooperating in Memphis and Nashville to match assistance program lists with state employment and other records, local welfare offices received a large number of phone calls from people asking to be removed from Food Stamp rolls because they had just found work.

In Illinois a recent effort by the State Employment Security Agency (ESA) and the U.S. Immigration and Naturalization Service to stop illegal aliens from receiving unemployment benefits by verifying their eligibility caused a dramatic drop statewide in the percentage of illegal aliens applying for assistance. Observers noticed applicants leaving ESA offices when they became aware that aliens were being asked about their residence status.

In a number of respects, many say that the development of computer matching techniques has actually lessened the threat of invasions of personal privacy by the government. For one thing, computer matching makes it possible to use large, separate, and disparate databases and files to prevent and detect error and fraud. This reduces pressure for some kind of central or national database, which might prove subversive of privacy.

Another consideration is that computers are considered to be much less intrusive with regard to individual privacy than people are. Government departments and agencies have the responsibility under law to protect the integrity and contain the costs of government programs they manage by preventing misuse, error, fraud, and waste. If government employees had to routinely read through individuals' file records to do the kind of comparisons and checking that computer matching accomplishes automatically, there would be infinitely more likelihood of invasions of privacy and much less confidentiality. The possibility of the misuse of information would be enormously increased because many more people would routinely have to have access to a great deal of information. Machines process file data quickly. They pick up and print only items that match. Machines do not recognize the names of friends, relatives, or neighbors. Machines do not have individual curiosity, do not tell interesting anecdotes about people, and do not gossip. In these respects, they are much more secure with respect to personal privacy than most people are.

POINT SHEET

SAMPLING FOR MODERN AUDITING: UNDERLYING LOGIC AND PRACTICAL TECHNIQUES

Before Taking Any Sample	Determine what is being tested.
	Why is it being tested?
	What is considered an error?

What will be done with the test results?

Good Sampling Techniques
A Basic Three-Part Rhythm

Do your thinking first.

Next, start doing your sample.

Last, begin assessing your work.

Saying This Differently

Know the important differences between probability and judgment samples.

Know procedurally how valid samples are drawn.

Know procedurally how results can be projected without distortion.

Two Broad Types: 1. Probability Samples (The Real Workhorse)

Descriptive analysis (background narrative).

Probability: another word for predictability.

Any probability sample is valid at a given confidence level. Samples of 200 or more will sustain dollar adjustments between parties.

Scientific predicates need a good, clean universe (if not, stratify the population until clean). Random selections require precise agreed-to terms as to what is and is not an error. Note: This whole process is related to quality control.

2. Judgmental (Nonprobability) Sampling. Note: More subtle, not fully scientific, harder to defend, very useful if done right

Under controlled circumstances, a sample of one may be valid—to prove a point.

Similarly, a "fishing around" sample may be reliable—if interpreted correctly.

For purposes of evidence, fraud cases may need only a judgmental sample of one.

Judgmental sampling is very useful in discerning a trend, or a "feel" for the situation.

It can be combined with probability samples or a stop-and-go technique.

Four Related Concepts of Probability Sampling: Three Main Averages.

The question is, Which to use? Whichever is most useful or most descriptive of the situation; never use the term *average* without defining the type used.

Averages:
measures of dispersion for normal distribution and probability distribution.

Arithmetic mean:
In general, it is the division of a sum of values by the number of values. Be careful, though–it is "pulled" in the direction of extreme values.

The median or middle value is less affected by any extremes.

The mode is the "most prevalent" value and tells which item came up more than any other. Caution: that's all it does.

Measures of Dispersion

Simply put, dispersion is the variation in the data being studied.

It also describes the significance of differences in the data field.

It can be used to measure the reliability of an average.

In mathematical terms (a shorthand of sorts) dispersion is called the "standard deviation."

There are other gauges like the "range," which is the difference between the largest and smallest values. But the range doesn't give useful information about the dispersion of the intervening values. The standard deviation overcomes this objection.

Normal Distribution

A normal distribution is simply the familiar bell-shaped curve.

If the universe under study is normal, then valid inferences can be drawn.

For example, we can tell the percentage of items within a specified distance from the mean.

If the universe is not normal, then special handling is required, including better stratification.

Probability Distribution

Defined as a listing of possible outcomes of the sample and the probability of the occurrence for each outcome.

Many classes: The two main classes are binomial and normal.

The binomial probability distribution has only two categories, like "heads or tails," each independent of the other.

The normal distribution requires an infinite number of outcomes in the experiment.

More Types

Unrestricted samples.

Stratified random samples.

Cluster samples.

Multistage samples.

Acceptance samples.

Discovery samples.

Interval samples.

Dollar-unit samples.

To Illustrate (A Step-By-Step Instruction)	
Define *What*	For this Point Sheet illustration, answer 100,000 paid travel vouchers.
Define *Why*	Your survey indicates that many of these vouchers contain errors.
Define *Error*	Error is defined as an underpayment or an overpayment of travel costs of whatever size.
Establish *Sample Size*	A minimum of 200 is required, owing to possible legal ramifications.
Determine *Method Of Selection*	Use 200 random numbers (ranging from 1 to 100,000).
Working With the Test's Results	Consult an appropriate random numbers table in any good sampling text (assume for the illustration that you are after 95% confidence level). At a 95% confidence level, the random numbers table shows that the *actual* error rate for all 100,000 travel vouchers is somewhere between 14.7 and 26.2%, with a midpoint indicated estimate of 20% (40/200).*
Assessment of Situation for the Report	It depends on the auditor's judgment as to the relative seriousness of the situation.
Computer Cross-Matching	It's not true sampling, but rather a 100% sweep of data. It entails machine comparison of computer-stored data. It's fast and usually quite accurate, but it takes planning. Computer cross-matching handles enormous

*How do you interpret these results? By adding nothing to what we already said in any prior step: There is a 95 percent probability that the actual rate of error in the entire population is somewhere between 14.7 and 26.2 percent. The midpoint estimate is 20 percent. And that's all we can say! Can we assign a probability to the midpoint estimate? No! Probability statements pertain only to the lower limit (14.7 percent) and the upper limit (26.2 percent).

amounts of data effortlessly with no human fatigue factor.

Can successful samples be drawn from the 100% sweep—for ease of additional or truncated study? Of course, that's the main objective of computer matches.

9

Computer Auditing: Getting a Handle on this Increasingly Vital Subject

The modern auditor's world has been made infinitely more complex by the now widespread use of ultra-high-speed, high-capacity microcomputers using unbelievably small recording chips. Like an ever darkening horizon, they must be approached understood, and reckoned with by every practicing professional. The checking of security methods, operating controls, programs, and computerized transactions must not be left to computer wizards (who tend to keep secret the mysteries of their electronic gadgetry) just as (1) writing clear, concise findings and reports need not be relegated to literary magicians, and (2) devising and using proper sampling methods and evaluations should not be sloughed off to special staff members with a penchant for higher mathematics.

There are four main lines of thinking that I will discuss from several angles: First, the fantastic nature of the technology itself, second, how computer wizards tend to keep their wizardry to themselves; next, the high organizational vulnerability of computer operations; and last, the gross lack of experience (or confidence) by the average auditor in this arena. I will also offer the reader some new ways of looking at the adequacy of automatic data processing (ADP) internal controls in place.

THE TECHNOLOGY FACTOR

As the computer revolution spreads, computer expertise is no longer concentrated in a relatively few "computer rooms." With the development of the integrated circuit (a complete electronic circuit on a small silicon chip), computer capacity and availability have soared and prices plunged. As a result, computers have spread throughout the country in large and small offices and the home. One serious problem with this widespread availability is *networking*, which permits everyone to get into the act with few if any audit trails to analyze and retrace transactions.

Here are some examples.

With electronic fund transfers (ETF) or instant banking, funds are transferred electronically (no paper) from checking and savings accounts using computer technology. The most visible feature of this is the automatic teller. Put your ID card in, punch in your personal ID number, and voila, deposits are accepted, funds are transferred, bills paid, and cash may even pop out in little bunches. How much money is being handled electronically? Some estimate a staggering $500 billion a day, but by the time the reader gets this far, it may well be estimated at $600 or more billion a day.

Eastern Airlines' ticketing network, one of several such networks, links various computers in Miami and Charlotte, North Carolina, with thousands of ticket agents, flight operations, and internal business operations terminals. The other airlines, domestic and foreign are all very similar.

The federal government alone has over 30 major telecommunications networks in the nonmilitary sector. (Who knows what the military and security agencies have at their beck and call.) Terminals at SSA field offices are used to input beneficiary data to hasten claims processing. The IRS has a dozen computer installations nationwide to handle tax data. Moreover, the two agencies are planning a data exchange to find missing taxpayers (all done, of course, within the protective limits of the Federal Privacy Act).

At the stock market, with computerization and computer terminals around the country, a 70 to 125 million-share exchange is now just a very ordinary trading day. Compare this with Black Tuesday's then all-time high of 16.4 million shares traded, considered in 1929 to be a staggering total.

Even home computer users are getting in on the networking act. Millions of units are expected to be in use in the near future. Telecomputing Corporation of America is offering the home user a networking service called Source for instant access to the UPI news wire, a vast array of stock and commodity marketing data, and computerized shopping. Audit problems can and do abound.

Tiny, household-sized computers can now handle what only very large pieces of equipment formerly could do. In 1976 there were an estimated 1500 personal-sized computers available or being used. In 1981, the supply increased to over 500,000. Anyone can take a guess what the total will be in the future. High school students and general office personnel wanting to raid data banks now have almost casual access to readily available equipment using widely known techniques. The potential for widespread computer fraud or abuse is obviously multiplying geometrically.

The "hard paper" that is usually relied on to support audit conclusions and criminal investigations is disappearing. While rules governing evidence are already undergoing reevaluation, federal and local legislators are not sure about what real impact any new legislation they consider, or pass, may have on many facets of computer security.

There are very few useful, or adequately described, information banks to help one gain insight into how abuses have specifically occurred in the past. Losses have been estimated by some experts at over $3 billion annually, but no one really knows. Secrecy generally prevails, in part, because CPAs do not routinely disclose whether their clients have been defrauded. Such nondisclosure is looked upon as a means of protecting clients from adverse publicity. Even if they were identified—because criminal activity required public disclosure—precisely how the fraud occurred and who perpetrated it are at best vaguely described in professional literature. CPA firms often display a whole array of mixed signals concerning their responsibilities, both to the profession, and to the public, for abuses affecting their clients.

Traditional and standard cut-off bank reconciliations, a prescribed and significant audit step, are rarely, if ever, employed by auditors checking federal, state, or local operations. The checks are issued but are never examined individually or compared physically to see that they agree with the journals of original entry. Related computer runs are merely tabulated to show a listing of total disbursements and payees versus authorized recipients. Endorsements are scrutinized only in very special (mostly criminal) cases. No examination is regularly made to ensure that checks are not issued without original and validated journalized records. This routine audit step—required by AICPA standards in the private business world and also required by GAO standards—isn't done! What's worse is that for practical purposes, there is an open-ended checkbook with no practical limit on the cash available in the public sector's coffers available to unauthorized and unscrupulous persons. And further, most computer systems do not provide any clear trail that would allow unauthorized outputs to be tracked to the individuals who initiated faulty transactions.

This entire situation is becoming compounded in the entire private sector as more and more banking institutions are truncating the returned cancelled checks procedures. That is, they are merely issuing their business patrons a monthly computerized tabulation check that summarizes the paper and electronic transfers going through their system. The actual cancelled checks are not being returned. Clients (and auditors) cannot, without special arrangement, perform their usual scrutiny of endorsements, signatures, proper amounts, and payees to tell if they agree with disbursement journals.

Let me illustrate what the auditor is up against in the everyday workings of a computerized accounting setup. Consider the ordinary aspect of lost or mislaid forms, documents, or any data that need to be posted. In an organization's precomputer days, lost material always took on an attribute of randomness. This invoice was mislaid, sent to another clerk for reverification, and never retrieved; this bill was inadvertently dropped in a wastebasket, and so on. Whatever the specific reason, the pattern was one of randomness–one form here, one document there, a few today, some tomorrow. The "materiality" of what could go wrong was limited.

But with the speed and storage capacity of a computer-based data system, a firm could literally "lose track" of a million transactions in 5 seconds of inappropriate runs. Formerly, an office would have to have a truck pull up and have three men remove, say 15 file cabinets of material to equal what a careless clerk (or a deliberate abuser) can take away or lose (electronically) in a few seconds. And what's worse, there are often inadequate duplicate data banks in cases like these. To illustrate in plain language, a data reel, for example, weighs less than 3 pounds–and can store over 3 million records. It can easily be inadvertently bumped off a table by a member of a night cleanup janitorial crew into a wastebasket. Floppy disks are a new form of the problem.

Therefore, as a basic, underlying concern in any review of a computer operation, auditors must consider process security against ordinary inadvertence that has the potential to be superdestructive.

Speaking about actual computer abuse, here are some flashy examples, cut down to size, that have previously hit the press.

A "bright young high school student" found some discarded computer printouts and operating guides in Pacific Telephone and Telegraph's trash. They enabled him to piece together how to access the Pacific Telephone computer system through a phone terminal. With further rummaging, he was able to find out how equipment was ordered by field locations from central inventory. A couple of years later, he decided to break into the system and go into business for himself. He proceeded to order various pieces of equipment for delivery at various coded job sites, usually late at night. (One delivery was made to a manhole at 2 a.m.). He was so successful, he built a company of 10 people with a 6000 square foot warehouse and misappropriated over a million dollars worth of equipment before being stopped. Since prosecutors could only prove he obtained $5000 worth of equipment, he was let off with a 40-day sentence and an $8500 fine. How was he caught? A disgruntled employee turned him in.

To enhance his job advancement, the best programmer on the staff of University Computer Company accessed a competitor's system to copy a sophisticated program. The program itself didn't cost that much to develop, but its competitive potential, as no one else had it, was placed at over a million dollars. The programmer was eventually traced through an error committed in gaining access to the competitior's computer, not by a security trap. His punishment: $5000 fine (which his company paid) and a suspended 30-day sentence.

A teller at Union Dime, a New York City savings bank, skimmed $1.5 million from large new accounts by making a simple computerized correction entry. His embezzlement was discovered when police investigated a gambling parlor he frequented and questioned the source of his betting money. His sentence: 20 months, of which he served 15.

The *New York Times* of January 2, 1983, recounted the tale of two Princeton University students who began using the university's main computer to exchange electronic mail. "Every few days I'd write her a little note, and when I'd log on, there would usually be a note for me," one student recalled. "It was just chit-chat."

Over time, the notes became increasingly personal. The two students, who had been casual friends for several years, developed a romantic relationship. "We had never really talked to each other," the other student said. "We started writing letters and then flirting in the letters. I don't think we could have done that in person. The computer bridged the gap."

Playing Cupid was certainly the last thing in the mind of Princeton administrators when they invested in the computer system. But the incident is an example of the way the electronic revolution can alter social life at colleges and universities around the country—at considerable cost to the schools. Computer centers are replacing libraries as the focus of much academic and social activity. Electronic mail is affecting everything from faculty politics to relations between the sexes, and the possibilities for electronic snooping and misuse are posing new challenges to honor systems.

The computer is dramatically and profoundly changing our lives, our lifestyles, and the way business does business. And with change comes all means of challenges, including a reluctance to change.

Just a few days after the computer/Cupid story broke, practically every business section in the country carried the story about data theft laid to a former Federal Reserve Board economist. This 34-year-old was only at the E. F. Hutton Company for 10 days when he was caught tapping the Reserve Board's computer to obtain secret data about the nation's money supply. Money supply data, if available in advance of its release each Friday by the Federal Reserve, would be of tremendous value to anyone trading in stocks and bonds. Interest rates and yields of government securities and bonds often move up or down when changes in the growth rate of the money supply are reported.

COMPUTERS CAN READILY BE TAPPED

The computer at a large research center is accessed by a telephone number that is published and that, in any case, is known to former employees. Former users are also aware that account numbers consist of four letters or digits. Passwords consist of three letters or digits. After getting on the computer with a valid account number, which is relatively easy, the unauthorized user has merely to try (26 + 9) characters in each of three positions to get a valid password. (Note: the 26 + 9 comes from the 26 letters of the alphabet and the 9 digits.)

Though this could easily be tallied by hand, a person adept at electronics could program a small home computer and an automatic dialing machine to carry out the task for him. As I am writing this, the national news is describing how high school students "broke" into hospital research data–just to see if they could do it. Of course, the unauthorized usage of a particular account would appear on the proper user's bill one month later, and the proper user could change his password. But the unauthorized user could simply change to a different account at that point.

This problem could be prevented by having users of computer accounts change their passwords a minimum of once a week. Changing your password is a very simple procedure, involving only punching in a few lines when beginning a terminal session.

LESSONS FOR THE AUDITOR

Auditors should at least be conversant with relatively simple security inquiries to protect their clients.

What is common to these tales is this: Computers work as machines; people commit the fraud. What is also common is that the take can be large, and the punishment is usually light. None of these scams were detected during the course of an audit! A major reason, of course, has to do with the adequacy (or paucity) of management's own system of effective internal controls (which we will discuss in the next chapter).

The first lesson for the auditor is to stay cool. The basic objectives of a system audit, computerized or manual, remain the same. Management's internal controls must be reviewed and tested to see if they are effective. The records produced (however recorded) must be examined for accuracy and reliability. Nothing new here.

What is the auditor trying to accomplish in his review of any automated (EDP) system of records? The answer is: The objectives are the same as if operations were manually kept.

Internal controls–really working?

Physical safeguards–fully adequate?

Operations–economically and efficient?

Data–meeting mangements' operational needs?

Reports–accurate and descriptive?

These quetions should sound familiar. The main distinction is that our EDP environment causes the whole process to be many times more intense and vulnerable. For example:

Large losses are much more possible and can occur much more quickly. The fast-moving EDP machinery can be used to plunder whole sections of a company before the executive management knows what hit it (recently publicized bank frauds attest to this).

Even if not deliberate, inadvertent clerical or procedural mistakes can be very expensive (for example, customers can be routinely charged $.38 for an item that should go for $380 each). EDP machinery is rarely programmed to effectively stop these absurdities–or even recognize them as obvious mistakes that ordinary people would spot in an instant.

Companies experiencing equipment breakdown (no matter how briefly) cannot really function manually any more. (On a small scale, watch any large supermarket try to operate and maintain checkout counters without its computer terminals.) Even if they somehow keep hobbling through an afternoon's business, whatever happens to its high-geared inventory control, internally?

To be helpful, however, let's put the safeguards needed for computer security (another name for internal controls) into manageable, more familiar terms. With some clear thinking, imagination, and some knowledge of EDP processing, auditors can reach a conclusion as to whether each significant part of the accounting system is controlled. They can still provide reasonable assurance that the system is free of material weaknesses. With the present widespread proliferation of computers, what are the possibilities for abuse?

First, let's look at some areas where our attention should be focused—and in the process, cut the examples cited down to size. A researcher at a large university recently studied a great number of cases of computer fraud and detected a pattern to the schemes that were most frequently used. What he found was that accounting, inventory control, and disbursement functions (as one would expect) were the most popular areas for manipulative schemes—with transaction altering or addition, particularly in the input stream, being the most prevalent mode. It appeared, though, that there was less of a pattern by application area, that is, receivables, payables, inventory, billing, and so on. What did emerge was that the majority of computer frauds (at least those detected) were "old wine in new bottles." They were not particularly new or supercreative other than the fact that the *computer* was used to provide a smokescreen. It did a more effective job of covering tracks and confounding older, classical methods of detection.

Having said all this, the reader must share with me the notion (and, of course, built-in audit apprehension) that there is a whole new breed of mustangs coming through the pass—bright, young computer geniuses who are used to playing with electronic gadgetry. They do it in their own homes with the ease and familiarity that previous generations had with abacuses or comptometers (I wonder how many readers know what this pre-1940 wonder was). But they can be checked!

Internal controls for ADP systems fall into three general categories: management practices, physical security, and system security. Let's take a run through each of these areas, bearing in mind that the threat of the "human factor" also includes programming flaws, data entry errors, and other plain old human mistakes.

Many experts recommend that the first step is to start with a look at the mission and objectives of the organization under review and its reliance on ADP to achieve those objectives. They also say to read all prior related audit reports, both internal and external, to see what previous reviewers had to say. This goes without saying. Inventory the equipment, hardware, software, terminals, and the like, and apply my survey "eagle eye" approach.

Next, find out what kind of top-management oversight controls are in place: Is there an executive ADP management committee for planning equipment purchases and plotting software needs? (An organization should record what it has, and will have, in writing. This is basic accounting, of course, but as other authors have noted, with so many branches of an organization purchasing computers nowadays, some companies have really lost track of how many they have at any given time.) Are the organization's own internal auditors involved from the planning to the output? They should be. Are policies and procedures in writing?

What kind of organizational (operational) controls are in place? Because of the concentration of functions brought about by the computer, make sure the data processing function is really separate from other agency functions. *ADP* procurement should be separate from the programming departments as well. Do different people or groups handle systems analysis, application programming, acceptance testing, program change control, data control, systems software maintenance, computer files maintenance? What kind of authorization is needed for system and program changes?

What kind of personnel background check is made? Is there a personnel rotation plan in effect within the different functional areas in the ADP department? Again, is all this in writing? (With these questions, be thinking about how transactions can be altered, particularly in the input stream. Remember, various ways of separating duties means cross checking.) Look, too, to the user; Is he or she satisfied with the results? If not, why not? What are the problems? Who knows about them?

All too often computer- or ADP-related problems are kept in management's own ADP family and not shared or considered properly by the general executive group. This is a bad oversight that auditors should be alert to.

As for physical protection, what are the controls in place over the hardware, software, tapes, and disks to protect against natural disasters, power failures, sabotage, and other threats? Are duplicate files maintained in a separate, secure location? Are security devices changed frequently? Is risk analysis performed not only just before the approval of design specs for an installation but also whenever there is a "significant change" to the physical facility, hardware, or operating system software?

What are the system controls? Does the system software contain a complete audit trail feature that records all changes to application programs, including assigning ID's to the programmer(s) making the changes? Is there strict security over the passwords or authorization codes given out for on-line access? What about that on-line access? Are passwords changed frequently? Are users only able to access certain data? What about transaction logs for on-line use—namely, who accesses what? (This is part of a built-in software package.)

As you can see, the questions that can be asked are only limited by the imagination of the auditor. (And if you run out of questions you can always go to the General Accounting Office's 279-page compilation of checklists, questionnaires, and matrices for more.) For actually testing data, other tools are available, such as HEWCAS, HHS' (formerly HEW) *C*omputer *A*udit *S*ystem—a custom-made COBOL program to process computer files and to transfer to another file or print the data that the auditor decides he needs for his audit. (The auditor, of course, is still required to develop the correct audit approach and audit logic.) As for finding some of those flashy fraud cases discussed earlier, HHS was one of the first major government agencies to use whole sets of computer applications "to ferret out fraud, waste, and abuse." They're free. Ask for them.

In the final analysis, like almost every subject area touched on in this book, it will be the ingenuity and logic of the practitioner that will offer breakthroughs and practical tests in the modern audit environment. No one can tell you what the whole set of problems are likely to be. The computer part of this world may be the toughest challenge. You must be prepared to match wits with the computer's people. One of the most intriguing, perhaps the most promising, of all the new methods in this connection may well be computer matches (see Chapter 8). This technique uses the forces and giant capacity of one computer to penetrate and unlock the data embedded in another electronic maze—a form of "Komputer Karate."

Where does this leave our auditor? How can he evaluate the auditee's books and records on a timely basis and assert reasonable assurance of reliability. I would like to explore a very important concept at this point, one that can serve *any* auditor well in reviewing almost *any* computer system for both efficiency and security: *compartmentalization.*

A NEW AND LOGICAL APPROACH TO ADP REVIEWS

First, think of spy networks. What single process makes them, when well developed, generally invulnerable to penetration? It is the individualized cell approach! Breaking down one spy (on interrogration, if caught) or breaking into one whole clandestine operation (if exposed) does not usually destroy the whole interwoven organization. This same notion can be applied analogously and very neatly to the general study of computers in two ways. Thus, always consider the need for (1) physical security (compartmentalized hardware), and (2) process segmentation (separation of duties and functions).

Let's further discuss these two main aspects of compartmentalization.

1. *Physical Modularization.* This safeguard can take a variety of well-known forms (passwords, locked rooms, cryptological scrambling, separate air conditioning, heavy fire walls, storm protection, burglar-proof tape and reel storage, earthquake springs, dust filters, window-free buildings, human guards, patrol dogs, duplicate data banks, and so forth). All of these must be persistently, if not fanatically, adhered to by all employees, or they become merely fragile, false-comforting screens for everyone in the company—high and low.

2. *Process Modularization.* The much more subtle, more difficult, but far more potent second aspect of compartmentalization is "procedural security through separation of duties, processes, and checkout functions—all related to people." Right here is where real internal control begins and prematurely ends in the computer business. One of the most important facets of an effective review process is up-front, design study. Consider again the age-old logic used by spy networks the world over. If one cell breaks down or its secrecy is destroyed, the entire cellular network is not destroyed. In other words, no one (or one group of) operator, programmer, analyst, maintenance person, and so forth should have access to the whole process so that it becomes wholly vulnerable to abuse. Look for real separation of ADP functions in a similar mode. It should, of course, vary from place to place depending on the extent and complexity of the operations, amount of hardware, and the sheer volume of operations, which dictate the use of EDP equipment in the first place.

AUDIT REVIEWS MUST BE ON-LINE

If the function of audit is to be intrinsic and useful to the internal control processes, it must be on-line or timely in the examination of the ADP processes. Procedures have to be checked while they are happening, almost literally, in the EDP area. You cannot come in later and expect to be able to effectively check ultra-high-speed runs, printouts, and most data analyses. Arrangements have to be made and audit techniques have to be employed on a very current basis. Absolute timeliness is essential!

Samples have to be drawn almost as quickly as the data are generated, or the bookkeeping will literally get away from you. Computers keep updating current accounts and dropping off old entries. There are no ending control balances with starting points that have details showing all the additions and subtractions or debits and credits to any summary accounts. That's not to say that one could not reconstruct prior balances from the piles of daily runs, but at what a cost! Dealing with computers late can be analogous to trying to provide preventive maintenance to high-speed jet motors while in mid-flight!

Early audit involvement is needed here to see if all practical internal controls and possible checking points have been incorporated into the whole operation. This provides timely, before-the-fact, useful audit help.

Not only the up-front audit trail protective service but the "during" aspect of the review is also highly dependent on whether the audit effort is on-line. The only practical aspects of auditing computer operations *after-the-fact* is in the arena of computer matches.

COMPUTER MATCHING/KOMPUTER KARATE

Computer matching is a very interesting angle to the whole subject of computer auditing that is amazingly potent and useful. It can be theatrically described as a form of "Komputer Karate." That is, the muscles or analytical strength of the computer itself are brought into play to assist the overall audit function by simply unlocking the data of another computer, using the second computer's programming and database strength. In this manner, desired data can be sorted and put into certain acceptable parameters. Then, with some ingenious cross checks built into the programming, we can easily disclose what we deem to be aberrant items. These aberrances, or "raw hits," are now surfaced and listed in easy study patterns. Let me elaborate a bit on this modern powerful audit method, discussed in Chapter 8 part with regard to sampling.

Computer audit usage may be classified into three distinct yet overlapping phases. Primary audit use of the computer was previously confined to "extracting" computer records that met specified criteria. Examples of extracting are printing for review any records that show overtime hours in excess of some maximum, any two records that match exactly, or any record that has a negative balance that should be positive. It is apparent that the computer can do more. The entire audit profession in the 1970s started heavily to invest its best talent into using the computer itself to "audit" other computer records. The leader in this area was the Department of Health, Education, and Welfare; William Wilkerson and James Foster were the masterminds of a set of brilliant innovative techniques, many of which are in widespread use right now, in and out of government.

Essentially, the computer provided a fast, efficient, and accurate means of reviewing voluminous amounts of data that heretofore had to be done manually and often on a sampling basis. Laborious tasks that previously took days (e.g., review of paid insurance claims for duplicate payments) can be done in a few hours. Computerized programs, including screening, editing, scanning, and matching between lists, files, or data within the same list or file, are used to both verify the data and identify irregularities. The irregularities must then be examined or verified, either through further computer applications or manual investigation, to determine if fraud or error exists. The computer, therefore, is a tool for simplifying the detection and prevention of fraud or errors.

The use of computer matches has progressed to sophisticated screening and analysis techniques designed to disclose patterns of fraud, waste, or abuse. Matches now involve the comparison of two or more computer files to determine similarity or dissimilarity of the data, while computer "screens" look for patterns of behavior, illogical relationships, and prohibited practices within files. They are often used to determine a potential problem. The raw hits (i.e., information from two or more computer tapes that appears to be identical, similar, or contradictory) might then be matched against other computer files to determine actual error, fraud, or abuse.

One more piece of advice is when you audit a computer center, think like a manager and merge that type of thought with your technical computer knowledge. How do you think like a manager? That's the simple part. Think in terms of traditional management objectives. The merging process is simple, too, if you have done a good job in learning the technical aspects of computers. Let me give you an example. We all know that it is a good practice to make duplicate copies of important master files that are kept on a computer. The key word here is *important.* Which master files are important? Oh, I suppose one could exercise one's "judgment," but there is a better–a much better–way! Master files pertaining to a company's primary objectives are surely important. (How would you like to lose the only reliable file that records sales on accounts or the key coding on retail inventories?) Files pertaining to indirect support objectives should rank below those pertaining to primary functions. See how it works? It is, as I said, a convenient mechanism for logical thought.

I said that my objective was not an instructional text about the technical areas of computer auditing. I won't imitate many fine texts on that subject. My objective is to give you a simplified, generalized, and logical approach for effective computer auditing. Without a proper game plan, all the technical knowledge in the world is of little use. The approach is to first and above all *think like a top-level manager.* Then, if you don't already have it, get sufficient detailed technical knowledge. (None of that "confined to the classroom" knowledge or two-day refresher courses)—become a computer programmer! Junior high school students are learning programming every day. Why shouldn't you? And, if you think the small personal computer is just a fad, or programming is for the strictly scientific-minded, consider this: Major universities are requiring all freshmen to own a personal computer. Not a little hand-held calculator, but something like a 16-bit, 64K RAM rig with monitor and all. Next, blend your top-level management thinking with your technical knowledge. That's the key—the only key! I've described 4 audit areas. You might want to make 5, 6, 10, or 20 areas out of the 4. Fine, go ahead. But whatever you do, think like a top-level manager, learn the basics of computer programming, and, above all, blend your top-level management thinking with your technical knowledge.

I will end my discussion of computers and computer auditing with what one might call "The Commandments of Computer Controls," with about the same mix of Do's and Don'ts that should be borne in mind by all reviewers.

1. *Do* have an up-to-date and formal organizational chart and statements of functional responsibilities. A computer is a magnet—it attracts data—all kinds of data—from every department in the organization. People in the computer center are charged with making sure that data are processed accurately, swiftly, and economically. And that's why it's so important to have a good, strong organization with clear statements of who is responsible for what—all in writing. In a computer center, a slip-up at the wrong time might result in the unthinkable—lost data. People must know what they are responsible for in clear terms. A computer center is no place for guessing!

2. *Do* segregate incompatible functional responsibilities. Don't let computer programmers (who design and write computer programs) operate the computer—if you do, the

programmers have complete control; they can do anything they want with the input, such as adding say an extra $1000 to their paychecks, and you will have a hard time finding out that it happened (even if you think it happened and you look for it). Don't let computer operators have authority to change computer programs; if you do, you are back to the computer programmer–operator problem. Do require prior approval by management before a computer program can be changed. Do use passwords and account numbers to restrict computer access to only authorized persons, and protect those passwords and account numbers. Don't let your EDP personnel have authority to authorize transactions. EDP types are data processors and that's all they should do—process data after it has been authorized by someone else. If possible, do segregate the responsibilities for the design, writing, and application of computer systems.

All of this is just good thoughts on good internal control. The only thing I have done is to apply the old concepts of internal control to a computer environment. I haven't tried to make a fully itemized list. There are plenty of specialized check lists available—use them. But remember while you are reading and studying a check list, the concepts of good internal control haven't changed because of the computer—the only thing that has changed is how we apply the old concepts to the computer.

INPUT CONTROLS

1. *Do* be careful in transcribing documents that are to be processed by the computer because a computer is absolutely inflexible. It will process anything you give it blindly. If you, or anyone, enters 1000 in a place where it shouldn't go, guess what the computer will do! It will post it and figuratively snatch that 1000 like it were gold.

It won't even know, or care, that you made a mistake of gross dimensions.

2. *Don't* assume that every document that the system calls for processing by the computer will be processed by the computer. Documents get lost. You should set up some type of numerical or batch control to be sure that what you send to the computer gets there.

3. *Do* be very careful in designing the forms that will be used for transferring the data into a form the computer can read. Haste makes waste! And that is more true than ever when "Mr. Computer Nice Guy" gets in the picture. Carefully design your input forms to make them simple. Relatively low-paid clerks will run them into the records as they are.

4. *Don't* assume that your input files are important only to the person or persons who sent them to you. Protect them in a secure place. It is expensive to recreate data files. And much of the data are sensitive and valuable to "outsiders."

5. *Do* follow up on input records that the computer does not process. Something is wrong on every record that the computer does not process. Too often, thousands upon thousands of records get "lost" in this manner. Never forget, input records must be in the exactly correct format before the computer will process them. If the records are wrong, send them back to the originator and follow up to be sure that corrections are made.

6. *Do* build sound editing procedures into your computer programs to be sure that the computer or programmers cannot force-feed obviously incorrect data into the system. Here are some things to look for: overtime hours that exceed regular hours, excessively high rates of pay, two time cards for the same employee for the same pay period, inventory balances that show negative quantities

on-hand, Social Security numbers that are all zeros, and people's names that have numbers in them.

7. *Do* set up a quality control system to pinpoint people who continually make large numbers of errors in preparing input for the computer. This could be one of your most profitable tasks. Remember, most computers catch or are programmed to reject the most obvious errors. The ones that are not so obvious get through the computer and into your data bank with damaging results.

POINT SHEET

COMPUTER AUDITING

Four Main Reasons Why Subject So Explosive For Auditors

Technology itself fantastic

It's ultra-high-speed; things happen so fast auditors can be quickly left in the lurch unless their techniques are absolutely on-line.

It has enormous capacity. All of a company's data can be kept in a dozen tapes, reels, or disks.

Tiny portable computers make it possible for electronic transferring to be open to many.

Secrecy

Computer wizards tend to keep their wizardry to themselves.

Insiders

ADP "experts" can intimidate management.

Resist up-front built-in controls.

Auditors too often audit "around" computer operations rather than meet them head on.

Vulnerability

Whole chunks of a company can be plundered quickly.

Even if not deliberate but only inadvertent, so-called minor clerical mistakes can be very expensive (e.g., customers charged $.38 for a $380.00 item); humans spot absurdities—machines process them!

Companies experiencing equipment breakdown can't effectively function at all.

Lack of Experience: (the average field auditor has no confidence in his ability to control this arena.)

Present-day senior auditors or audit managers did not grow up with computers; they psychologically resist them and leave the area to others.

Both senior and junior audit personnel are not well versed in effective logical audit procedures and rely on computer audit packages developed by others.

Similarly, there is overreliance by audit managers on computer programmers for basic guidance in audit engagements.

Short Background. Some Descriptive Cases That Illustrate the Vulnerability of the Area (Some Sobering Thoughts)

Over $500 billion worth (or more) of electronic transfers occurs daily.

Millions of home machines will soon be in use.

Hard-copy records are disappearing.

Details useful to the auditor concerning previously found abuses are skimpy.

Some Examples (in Easy Language) of How Computers Are Used

Networking

Where used

Instant plastic banking card.

	Airline ticketing. SSA field offices. Stock markets, news agencies, and many others.
Where Abused: A Few "Flashy Public Examples"	Pacific Telephone: equipment theft. University Computer Co.: program theft. Union Dime: dollar theft. University: private use by students. E. F. Hutton/Federal Reserve: data theft. Research center password: security breach. The patterns of most frauds: old wine in new bottles.
Classic Audit Solution	Use traditional techniques–review and test. Ensure management oversight. Good physical controls. Good operational controls.
Important New Approach–Compartmentalization	Its concept is cellular. On-line testing is crucial under any computerized technique.
Staff Investment in Understanding Computer Operations: Must Be Extensive if Work Is to Meet Standards	The areas of ADP data-related cash receipts or disbursements are the most urgent from the viewpoint of vulnerability.

10

On-Line Auditing: How to Avoid the Deadly "Stale Rolls Syndrome"

One can easily defend the general proposition that timeliness is the key ingredient of successful, economical, and responsive auditing—auditing that meets all standards. Similarly, it can be shown that tardy, stale audit efforts lead to sloppy, uneconomical, and often faulty (at least in part) audit efforts. Accordingly, I would like to illustrate how these considerations—both the positive aspect of timeliness and the negative one of untimely efforts—are not only central to auditing but have easily recognizable counterparts in many facets of our every day business and social life.

First, what are the conceptual elements; what are the practical aspects of timely on-line auditing (the how-to) techniques; and where and how should they be used?

Second, what happens if auditors or audit staffs fall into the "Stale Rolls Syndrome." You will soon see why I use this familiar expression to describe "stale audits." First, though, let me discuss the entire subject in a general narrative form. (I refer you to my Point Sheet for a more structured text.)

Last, to help the reader translate the stale rolls concept into practical terms, I will illustrate with a number of mundane daily happenings.

American automobile manufacturers are now paying a steep price for not properly monitoring their assembly lines to correct production foul-ups as they were found. Interrupting assembly lines meant the loss of real dollars, but only for the short run. The general practice was to let the dealers' or the customers' own mechanic correct production errors and defects later after the car was delivered.

Japanese automakers had a diametrically different philosophy. They were determined to have an effective on-line quality control system that enabled them to spot defects or weaknesses as they occurred. This permitted (no, it encouraged) quick fixes as soon as defects were found and prevented things from getting worse. It served to protect customers from getting shoddy merchandise or outright lemons.

ON-LINE AUDITING

In a similar sense, this is what my suggested on-line auditing is all about. Timely and periodic checking of accounting and operational data should be done by both the auditee and outside auditor to ensure high-quality operations and recordkeeping. System weaknesses or excessive clerical mistakes, even under a good system, can be spotted early enough to minimize financial losses.

Why do we find it so important to stress and elaborate this seemingly basic and fundamental concept? Because most federal, state, city, and county auditors are at the present time reviewing old transactions, events that occurred anywhere from one to three years ago. Many private auditors don't review or check items less than six months old. More often than not, they audit to recorded figures after the balance sheet date. To a lesser extent, but still to a significant degree, internal auditors are also failing to practice current on-line auditing and management review technologies.

How does one answer the question, Why did the auditing profession got locked into testing old transactions in the first place? There are many reasons. The one most pertinent and persistent is the fact that many managing auditors and their staffs are forever playing catch-up football. Stale jobs need finishing and reviewing. They stack up to the point where needed review efforts related to new efforts are late before they get started. The bottlenecking usually occurs at the decision-making, supervisory level.

Poor work planning permits unacceptable, inaccurate, and wasteful practices to continue for undue periods of time before they are exposed and stopped. Unexpected material financial adjustments and negative budgetary surprises can easily occur.

The staleness of the disclosures make for unnecessary difficulties adjusting and correcting previous errors. Staleness is the key word. Discussing a straightforward and relatively uncomplicated concept (such as timeliness) puts an author in the seemingly uncomfortable role of explaining the obvious. But, this is apparently what's needed because untimeliness in the audit profession is not productive and leads to unnecessary risk taking, which is anathema to the audit process.

AS FOR STALE ROLLS

Permit me to digress and illustrate the fundamental and central point of *timeliness* from a real-life saga.

My wife and I have a young-in-heart friend whom we have known for many years (let us call her Gloria). Recently, while reminiscing together over some crisp, fresh, Sunday-morning breakfast rolls and coffee, Gloria talked about how her parents were doing and how they, too, loved to breakfast each morning on freshly baked rolls with cheese and hot strong coffee. Her mother (Mrs. F.) would go to the corner bakery each morning and buy two fresh rolls for herself and Gloria's father. But years and years ago, for reasons now forever lost, Mrs. F. initially bought four rolls instead of two. However, only two were eaten that morning. The next morning, beginning a long time ritual, two fresh rolls were bought. But there were the two left over from the day before. "Let's not waste them!" admonished Mr. F. Thus, the next morning and every morning afterwards, Mr. F. only bought two more rolls because that's what they ate—two rolls. But thinking they were being tidy and economical, they ate the leftover rolls first. Therefore, there were always two stale rolls to eat and two fresh rolls to save. Imagine, they ate stale rolls all their long married life simply because 40 some-odd years ago they were reluctant to throw away two stale rolls!

In the audit and more generally in the management business, we too often act on and review "stale" matters or accounts while problems in the more important current operations are left to harden. The on-line approach, which offers a feasible and practical way out of this stale-rolls audit dilemma, is administratively worked out along the following lines.

IMPLEMENTING ON-LINE AUDITS AND EXPECTED BONUSES

As a sort of joint venture between the auditee and the client, on-line auditing entails (1) targeting those auditees having a competent internal review staff, (2) identifying selected types of transactions to be covered (those usually susceptible to extrapolation from random probability sampling techniques, but judgmental sampling can also be used), (3) reaching a general understanding with the auditee on the degree and nature of participation by both parties, and (4) planning in advance, with adequate testing by both parties, the specific techniques to be employed. No two accounting systems are alike, nor are any identical businesses to be found.

Thus, as a first step, executive managers at the president, vice president, or owner level must agree to jointly participate with their chief auditors to use on-line techniques and bring the audit routine to a current base. This mutuality of interest, at high levels, is very important and must be made unmistakable to their respective organizations. Managers and auditors together must:

Define areas to be included in the on-line review and decide on when the work will begin.

Identify individuals who will be in charge and who will participate.

Decide how the on-line audit verification results will be reported to management or third parties and choose the method of follow-up that will be utilized to assess the adequacy of management's corrective action.

Prepare and test any needed computer programs for selecting the random sample.

Work out a trial run of areas to be included in the test and decide whether it should be one (or more) month's transactions, or perhaps a whole process. The client's internal auditors and/or CPA's then begin the on-line auditing. It is best to select and review transactions on at least a quarterly, preferably a monthly, basis. Current problems, in keeping with the concept, would be disclosed quickly, and thus could be corrected more easily.

There will be, as a natural end product, a minimum of budgetary surprises; the whole process practically ensures much smaller financial adjustments. Monetary findings, emanating from compliance internal auditing, will involve much fewer possible costs questioned. The errors cannot compound.

Any audit group, governmental or private, can maximize the use of its own resources, since the internal staff of the client are fully utilized to do its share. In many ways, the techniques employed embody the same ones used in a residency auditor situation. But using this approach, rather than relying solely on long-standing, in-house resident groups, avoids the fatal flaws of close, day-to-day familiarity and the related tendency toward overlenient criticisms. Similarly, it is not much different from the concurrent audit techniques now employed by many auditing firms whereby line items on the balance sheets, the profit and loss statement, and internal controls are tested periodically—principally by the client under CPA monitoring and methodical scrutiny. All this is done *during the operating year* and not under any severe year-end time constraints. This, of course, also lessens considerably the possiblility of unpredicted and disruptive major year-end adjustments. Clients, traditionally, have limited patience with auditors who spring major financial surprises on them.

A few illustrative methods may, at this time, be useful in this discussion. Take a few balance sheet items, for example:

Cash. The internal audit staff can intercept cancelled checks every month from the banks that still provide them (or computer entries) and systematically random sample a sufficient number of disbursements to enable a satisfactory checkout of the cash disbursement journal. CPA's can participate each month for one day. This will be a good early check if any aberrant or collusive disbursement practices are in progress. The most outstanding example of on-line techniques I can think of also relates to cash and ADP records. Some auditors checking banking transactions are literally testing them as they occur. They position themselves behind the scenes at the computer centers and run sample checks of debit and credit transactions concurrent with customers' orders or receipts. The electronic transfer society we live in necessitates this absolute, on-line technique.

Accounts Receivable. A random sample of shipping tickets, collated to sales charges and checked to accounts receivable, can be made each month. This would be better in some aspects than a year-end receivable verification (at least it could materially supplement it) because weaknesses would not go undetected for a year or more before correction.

Inventories. Physical inventory testing can be done on an almost continuous yearly basis with small samples currently checked to recorded receiving tickets and inventory balances.

Purchase prices can more easily be checked if done on a timely basis. Here also aberrances will come under early scrutiny. Physical inventories are really a snap if checked piecemeal and often during the operating year and not en masse in one grand, hysterical swoop by a team of disgruntled auditors on New Year's Eve or other fiscal cut-off times. Also, many analysts claim that counting 100 percent of all physical inventories injects more errors into the system than existed before because inventorying personnel become bored and fatigued with extensive counting chores and tend to become mentally and physically sloppy and less accurate. Therefore, a little bit, monthly or bimonthly, is just the right on-line medicine.

Payroll and Personnel Records. Perhaps the most productive of all possible on-line checkout possibilities is here. It is too late, and frequently impossible, to successfully check what personnel have researched, worked on, or developed if it is done in an untimely fashion. People cannot from memory be expected to reliably confirm what they physically did 5, 10, or 15 (or more) months ago, for example. Successful floor checks are also impossible to do unless they are planned, carried out, and checked concurrently, and at random, with the combined forces of the company's own monitoring team in concert with the outside independent auditors.

Receiving Function. Try to visualize how much easier it is to check receiving records (together with related purchase files and accounts payable entries) if they are sampled, checked, and verified from a precontrolled sampling technique as they occur, on the spot, and not three or more months later backwards through the accounts payable audit questionnaire process to suppliers' routes.

In summary, quick and reliable changes for the better are the main conceptual objectives of on-line auditing. Putting this concept into practice creates an effective early warning device for detecting system problems. Many operating managers are also convinced that timely audits are important steps toward better managing large government programs or private enterprises and for keeping inappropriate disbursements to a bare minimum. Most important, it significantly lowers the possibility of abuse or major error. This cannot be overemphasized in the modern business climate.

POINT SHEET

ON-LINE AUDITING

Timeliness a Key Ingredient of Successful Audits	Timeliness results in economical effort. It responds to a need for considering materiality. It is required by standards.
Tardy or "Stale" Audits Are Conducive to Faulty Work	Tardy audits may cause important data to be missed if reviewed after the fact. It is much harder to reconstruct accounts than currently test and analyze them. Tardy audits pile up the audit manager's or supervisor's desk with "old" work which is difficult to properly review. The field auditor is on another assignment. Tardiness leads to fraud or abuse (potential perpetrators have too much time).
Regarding the Various Phases of Audit Effort:	
Survey and Verification in General	If the auditor doesn't know what is currently happening, how can he be pragmatic or useful in recommending any change for the better? Also, auditee is in far better position to remember current happenings.

Reporting a number of benefits derived from timely results	Practical recommendations that are responsive to current needs. Since errors are caught early, the findings are relatively small in dollar impact, causing no budgeting dismay. Much greater management receptivity—again, smaller error, caught early, does not (psychologically) imperil management at all levels. The audit tolerance level is then under good control. Easier to "linguistically" handle by audit reporter. Items discussed are fresh in the minds of all parties affected. The auditor is not discussing ancient history.
The On-Line Formula: Move Away from Post-audits	Auditors are being forced to make more current audits, a long overdue development; the "why" is discussed. Problems with post audits: data go stale, problems grow and fester. On-line audits are timely plus . . .
Prior Experience with the On-Line Concept in the Government and the Private sector	Plenty of problems, no easy answers if you stay with post audit techniques.
The "Stale Rolls" Revelation	What to do with the old when you must switch to the new: Throw away a few stale rolls!
When You Have Decided to Go On-Line	Target your auditees; identify those whose audit staffs can help. Obtain support of top management for your proposed on-line work. Work out the scope, the type of sampling, and the staff to be made available to you. As for staffing an on-line audit function, consider using any or all of

these: residencies, internal audit staff, comptroller staff, analysts.

Related Practical Aspects of Quality Control (Areas Where On-Line's Techniques Are Imperative)

Security checks (continuous observations) are mostly in areas related to cash handling or other small, portable valuables (gems, securities, etc.). Examples:

Computer security and ADP data.

Gambling tables.

Postal stations.

Mint operations.

Jewelry exchanges.

Diamond markets.

Restaurants, bars.

Gas stations.

Race tracks.

Banking transactions.

Payroll and floor checks cannot wait for later document scrutiny; they must be done concurrently.

Cops on the beat represent on-line protection. Super sleuth, after-the-fact detectives are not really useful in preventing crime.

Military training readiness assessments can only be done on the spot (reviewing reports is not effective).

Manufacturing operations in general can only be quality tested on a beltline basis in the production cycle (e.g., the Japanese auto industry).

Inventories lost or taken? who knows? On the other hand, organizing and testing in an on-line timely manner all throughout the fiscal period give management and auditor real control over the entire process.

Studies show that 100% physical inventorying frequently injects

	more errors into the system than existed before.
	Physical means for a 100% count often are lacking (counters, fork-lift trucks, time to do it all at once while shutting down operations).
	Fatique is a negative factor.
In Conclusion: The Audit Begins	
The Preliminaries	Strictly follow traditional audit approaches, here's added insight into what you may consider
The survey	The traditional approach. The "good vibes and bad vibes" syndrome is explored.
Verification	On-line begins paying off with insights into such ultrasensitive areas as inventories and any cash-related transactions. Warnings on electronic transfers.
A Question of Standards:	Overall, are they being met with postaudit approaches? (not according to the standards).
In a Nutshell What Is Called For	Judgment of auditors, evidence requirements, ethics, professional conduct, adequate reporting.
Meeting Standards through On-Line Audits	The materiality factor sampling techniques using on-line checking, and avoiding fraud by using front-end audit controls.
	Improvements in reporting through use of on-line attributes.

11

Output-Oriented Examinations: A Role for Auditors

Compare modern sports and intellectual endurance records with records of just 50 years ago. Who could visualize then running a mile in less than 4 minutes, or pole vaulting over 15 feet, much less 18 feet! How about the interesting world of chess—modern chess wizards can play over 50 games expertly, simultaneously, and blindfolded, with total recall, an impossible feat in the 1800s. But powerful new tools are here to help us come closer to reaching our mechanical and analytical limitations.

Untiring computers now deal with masses of tedious and repetitive processes with which the human brain cannot or will not cope. We now also have computerized audit techniques to probe deeply into the previously untapped reservoirs of data stored by computers. Working with the mass of data being tabulated or churned out by modern-day computers has heretofore posed formidable mechanical problems for auditors. New technology, though, can largely overcome such problems.

But our traditional audit attitudes and approach have also limited our reasoning capabilities. Traditionally, we have emphasized and concentrated on "inputs," management processes, functional controls, administrative practices, and so forth. This approach is changing. Auditors are beginning to direct part of their efforts at "outputs" by attempting to gauge actual results against expected aims for whatever program activity or function is under examination.

There now exists in many management circles a very receptive attitude to this idea. This change in approach is bothersome to many auditors and insufficiently understood by some program managers. But it is important to move from the traditional audit posture—involving fiscal management and compliance with program or organizational requirements—to one that considers, as a high priority, an assessment of the *accomplishment* of business objectives. This is not to say that examination into the reliability of fiscal records and compliance with required management policies are not of the utmost importance.

There are systematic and practical ways of moving in this new direction. They do not require esoteric audit methods but rest on modernizing well-understood, fundamental audit techniques. Understanding and applying these basics may well make for truly sophisticated and disciplined auditing that can respond to management's needs in both administering and evaluating large and complicated operations in the entire business community.

Let us take another look at the review process. Businesses of all sizes are concerned with how well they are doing in comparison to their peers, in relation to their overall public or private accountability, and certainly, in measuring up to their own particular financial expectations. What are some of the fundamental audit techniques called for here?

The first that comes to mind, and perhaps the most important, is information gathering. Many observers of the auditing profession have maintained that one of the auditor's main purposes in the management cycle is to provide unbiased and useful information presented in a disciplined and controlled fashion. If auditors have any single characteristic that distinguishes them from other professionals in the management field, it is their strong stomach for detail. Also, auditors have a knack for ferreting out and displaying relevant and meaningful information. I am not sure whether these traits are inherited, and that, therefore, auditors naturally gravitate into this field; or whether these characteristics are inculcated by repetitive practice after they get into auditing. Either way, the abilities germinate at the academic level and are reinforced throughout the auditor's professional career.

If we accept the basic premise that data gathering is one of the prime functions of the auditor, then many of his (or her) activities fall into a consistent pattern. Attesting to the accuracy and reliability of financial and administrative records, for example, is only possible after sufficient related facts have been accumulated to enable the auditor to report on them.

In any event, the techniques for getting information have vastly improved. Some of us still remember the old ways. One piece of nostalgia involves what might be termed "backwards testing." This procedure (with minor variations on the theme) goes something like this: (1) You have a feeling that errors are probably occurring in a certain area; (2) You scratch around until you find some, (3) You write up appropriate journal entries, or reports, to correct the specific errors found, and (4) You tell management all about the big procedural breakdown.

This technique gave way to the "sample month" method. It seemed like auditors always tested April and October. I'm not sure, but I think this was done because these two months seemed economically representative; they did not relate to possible accentuated seasonal extremes (Christmas or summertime). Also, government agencies that are involved in reviewing sales tax reports and income tax matters seemed to think these two months were appropriate for adequate sampling. Therefore, accountants often picked these months for special attention.

We later moved from the April-October syndrome to the old familiar "10 percent method." Every tenth voucher or transaction was tested for accuracy. Ten percent of anything seemed comfortable as a proportion.

In any event, we finally moved to scientific statistical sampling procedures, a great improvement. Within designated tolerances, we can now offer reliable opinions on the entire universe of data examined and make projections in a fairly accurate fashion. If the procedures are used correctly, they help auditors to come up with accurate and balanced reports.

There are now, however, ultramodern methods that give the auditor the capability to test almost unlimited quantities of data quickly and efficiently through the use of generalized computer audit programs. These programs not only provide reliable audit data based on computer-generated statistical samples but can search for duplicate transactions, verify the integrity of information fields, and, if warranted, examine the database in its entirety. Auditors can now gather vastly more useful data through generalized computer audit program techniques. We no longer need to guess at the number of potential errors. The potency of audit-based information is thus greatly enhanced. Auditors can tell exactly what has happened. The ability to analyze and relate all the common-based data reduces the amount of material that heretofore appeared inconclusive. Of course, use is limited to organizations that have computer-based data, but since more and more operations are being computerized, our field is enlarging constantly. The ability to use computer audit techniques puts the auditor in a position to help management to an extent undreamed of a few short years ago. The challenge is unmistakable.

Consider the overall area of concern (at least in government or big business circles). The sheer size of the problem makes sophisticated data gathering meaningful, pertinent, and essential. Recent studies point out that private philanthropic and public social welfare expenditures amounted to more than $2000 per person in the United States. Public social expenditures, as defined in the study, included cash benefits, services, and administrative costs of all programs that were of direct benefit to individuals and families. These expenditures are a high percentage of national product.

These enormous expenditures elicit the question, What are the benefits? Before one answers, I feel one must deal with the criteria. What is considered good? Most auditors agree that criteria for measuring program, business, or organizational results in "soft" industries are often insufficiently delineated or at least imperfectly stated. Many objectives, even standards, are actually only hypotheses whose tentative nature precludes accurate derivation of criteria.

In the private sector that deals with nonsocial products, thoughts about criteria area, oddly enough, more easily shunted aside. Most businesses are considered effective if they make profits—very effective if profits continue to rise. How does one determine, however, if they should have profited more from the capital, market potential, and know-how the firm possessed? And are short-range results obtained from long-range detriment? One need hardly look further than the automobile industry to illustrate this point.

Auditors need not be fearful of getting into these heady areas. Anyone who can contribute is usually welcome to speak. It probably has not been said often enough, "it's easy to make decisions when you have few or no alternatives!" More information reduces the number of alternatives—logically, thus easing the way to deciding best courses.

Maybe intuition starts to take over at this point. It has also often been said that heads of large corporations base their hardest decisions on so-called "gut feelings" about things.

The ability to interpret and act on hunches, correctly and consistently, usually marks the successful organization president! But the need for hunches usually stems from the paucity of good data, which are pointedly missing in uncharted and broad major decisions areas. Why not try to help narrow the gap? Why not assist in moving intuitive judgment closer to informed opinion making? Independent (especially intelligent and worldly) auditors are in an increasingly unique position to do this.

POINT SHEET

People and Auditors, Using Only a Minute Part of their Brain Capacity, Have Concentrated on "Inputs"	Untiring computers can now pick up the slack.

	Outputs are now being given attention.
	New management is receptive to this changed attitude.
	Output orientation should not be bothersome or mysterious to auditors.
	Auditors can handle needed details.
	Computers can now do much of the raw analysis.
	The very size of modern concerns dictates attention to "outputs."
Subject of Criteria Is Intrinsic to Understanding	What is considered to be a "good" operation?
	It's not enough to have profits, even if on the upswing; maybe more income should have resulted from a better analysis.
	Informed data collection reduces the number of poor alternatives.

12

Cost Accounting: Easy Does It

Auditing cost accounting operations involve special considerations. Foremost is a journeyman's knowledge of the logic behind the mechanics of cost accounting. Attaining such proficiency is at present a very ponderous process, and one that may be viewed as a partial waste of time. The average business administration graduate majoring in accounting nowadays undergoes pretty much the same routine curriculum as have others over the last 40 years. Accounting courses typically include many semester hours of very stilted cost accounting instruction culminating in bone-crushing examples of complicated job order and manufacturing plant studies. I can still remember (with dismay) the awful brick manufacturer who produced 182 sizes and qualities of bricks, with various ceramic and tile sidelines. Cost problems were built (brick by brick) around him to see if you could figure out what the various products really cost to produce and whether each separate sales level was profitable. Granted, this information is essential to the owner or manager of the brick plant. But students need not spend whole semesters learning the intricacies of costing brick manufacturing. The point is that there are almost endless varieties of cost accounting situations depending on the nature and needs of particular manufacturers. Students, who later become journeyman accountants (or auditors), can cope with any of them when the need arises by understanding fully the lowest common denominator of the general concepts involved.

A CASE IN POINT

Let me illustrate all this point by describing a cost study involving an eight-room house. The housewife wants to have the interior repainted; her husband is busy. The housewife calls the local paint contractor and tells him what she wants. "Can you quote me a price?" He will probably not do it over the phone—and shouldn't if he is sharp or reliable. He will insist on seeing the house first. The painting contractor then makes a trip out to the house to see its condition—the size of the rooms, its location, how far it is from the business office, and anything else that might affect the performance of the work.

Then previous experience comes into play. The contractor's firm has painted eight-room houses before. He also knows that an average house room takes two cans of paint, if it only needs one coat, and one painter working one-half day to paint it. Therefore, an eight-room house would need 16 cans of paint and 4 man-days. This is, of course, the average painter's productivity quotient, not that of the superfast or barely marginal journeyman.

Then the contractor totals up the other direct charges, such as the average wage of the painters, and such disposable items as the cost of brushes that wear out in the course of painting the eight rooms, masking tape, thinners, and so on. Then comes the critical part—overhead or indirect charges. The manager must estimate payroll taxes, fringe benefits, pension plans, workmen's compensation, insurance, auditing, rent, utilities, finance, and accounting—all of which can be computed and allocated by using any number of bases.

One of the easiest bases would be labor hours. Compare all the labor hours in the whole work force and then allocate overhead expense, including rent, insurance, automobile cost, stationery and supplies, depreciation on the fixed assets, and everything else that you can throw in. This charge to the customer constitutes a very simple rate for indirect cost and entails a simple percentage of how much of the total business cost is applicable to this job. By applying the overhead and a factor for profit, the contractor can have a solid basis for estimating the cost of any given job that would return all of his expenses plus a reasonable profit. This is the critical *first stage* of cost accounting estimating. One can expand this procedure to a whole plant where this type of operation exists in different cost centers in the same way. It also applies in the case of a redecorating firm, including painters and paper hangers from all over the city. Add any number of complications or extra factors; it's all the same.

As for our story, the housewife agrees to the total price, the contract is set, and two painters start on Monday morning. At the end of 2 days, they should be finished. A good supervisor, plant manager, or owner-entrepreneur would not wait 2 days to come and see whether the job is finished or to ask about its progress. He would slip by to observe results at the end of the first day. What would he expect? He would expect four rooms to be painted, eight cans of paint to be used up, and a normal usage of supplies. Suppose he comes by and finds only one room painted, three cans of paint used, and brushes worn out extraordinarily fast because of the roughness of the walls. Obviously the estimate would have been wrong.

Because the actual cost was inaccurately computed, the indirect cost was underapplied. The supervisor's accounting (or accountant) has to make a simple adjustment to reflect the fact that now it will take more cans of paint and more man-days to finish the job. The amount of the difference is underapplied cost to this job and enters into the firm's accounting (historical) experience. The business can more intelligently estimate future jobs. All of this, of course, depends on the journeymen's working in the normal fashion (no faster or slower than what is expected of them). If their pace is different, then a new norm must be considered for future work.

Suppose the paint foreman visits a similar job and the same thing happens except that after 1 day even less work is accomplished. Then it's time to take a look to see whether men are shirking or the estimates are again understated. This is the intrinsic process of cost accounting. One must establish a direct cost norm, base it on historical experience, set a separate composite norm for the indirect cost, all in a logical and simple fashion. Whether we are describing a simple paint job, or a complicated factory with process manufacturing and many products, the procedure is intrinsically the same. Keep track of differences in a systematic way, but don't go overboard trying to master details.

THE SUBTLETIES OF COST ACCOUNTING

Of course, I have greatly understated the complications that might ensue. Knowing the basics, however, and understanding the logic behind direct and overhead applications will serve the average internal auditor, or the average cost accountant, in good stead–no matter what cost accounting situation he or she runs into. To spend semesters studying a whole variety of past complications is a gross waste of time because one never (well, hardly ever) runs into the same cost accounting situation twice.

Having said all this, what then are the audit implications? It would seem now to be self-evident that a high incidence of missed estimates results in numerous changes in applied costs or overhead adjustments. This is the key for the auditor. Conversely, if you see reliable and stable entries over a period of time, then the system is probably well constructed.

The process of allocating expenses to any set of cost units is not, by any means, a fixed and stereotyped routine. For example: When a person says that his shoes cost $50, he probably is refering to the purchase price of the shoes. One would not consider the time spent in getting to the shoe shop, the gas and oil of the car or its depreciation, the time spent finding and fitting the right shoe for a particular purpose, and so on.

But if a person bought these shoes to sell to someone else, then this would be an entirely different matter. The invoice price would have to be adjusted for freight, buying expense, accounting costs, building depreciation, related salary expenses, indirect costs, taxes, and so on.

The need for a lowest common denominator is evident when dealing with cost accounting. The variation in cost concepts can be illustrated by contrasting the economist's use of the term *cost* with that of the general accountant. The accountant would include in the cost the entire invoice price of purchased materials; the economist, however, would exclude from cost the "profit" of the seller. Gains by the seller are not cost in an economic sense, except for such portion of book profit as represents a return to owner-managers for the use of capital or for services rendered. Economists are concerned with the cost to society, not to the enterprise–sacrifices (human or entrepreneurial) included in cost are different in the two points of view.

The economist, on the other hand, would include in cost things that the cost accountant would not; the cost accountant includes only financial values, whereas the economist must include such "social" costs as are pertinent to his problem, including unemployment, industrial mortality, disease, and the like. These are outside the boundaries of individual enterprises and are not directly, or usually, measurable in monetary terms. Yet they must be included in economic cost, since from the social point of view they are casualties of the productive process representing a loss of social assets, even though it would be difficult or impossible, under most circumstances, to assign a value to them.

So, all in all, accounting for cost, by any definition, is a complex and varied process. Nevertheless, understanding some of the underlying concepts is not only relatively easy, but is all that is needed in most cases to implement specific auditing applications.

POINT SHEET

COST ACCOUNTING

Auditors Should Not Spend Great Amounts of Time Studying Cost Accounting Methods	The varieties of methods are almost endless.

Understanding just the basic logic would serve the auditor well in most situations; that is:

Develop a historic estimate for labor, materials, and overhead.

Isolate indirect cost pockets (really not hard to do).

Check the results in a timely fashion throughout operations.

Make quick adjustments as needed to your rates. Be able to distinguish between the elements of cost accounting and broader-based economic costs.

13

The No-Product Dilemma

Industry and government spend uncounted billions each year in new, basic research and development. Yet there have been few public audit reports published and fewer private reports available or prepared that evaluate the effectiveness and the efficiency of these expenditures or even state whether they comply with basic, organizational policy or intent. Why has this serious void occurred?

Consider the performers or sponsors of basic research—foundations, universities, charitable organizations, social programs, fraternal groups, the Department of Defense, religious affiliations, hospitals, drug manufacturers, and so on—the list is extensive.

The assessment process calls for logic, the application of good sense, and a disciplined approach to the examination of the administrative practices of the research organization under review. Since auditors have their fair share of logic and good sense, their training and persistence should enable them to handle the last requirement well. Before proposing a useful methodology for auditors (or any reporter with good sense) in what is generally considered a difficult assignment, I must ask readers to consider three basic assumptions, then judge for themselves whether they are logical and fundamental.

First, all research is essentially a management gamble. Basic research is the riskiest gamble of all and covers the widest spectrum. Chances here are greater for economic loss than in applied or product research (where an identifiable item is being developed or produced for a specific end result).

Second, satisfaction with a research effort or a proposal to embark on a research effort because "expert peers" say it is good is not necessarily, by itself, a fully satisfactory management process.

Here are a few of the reasons:

Peers have personal biases. Final judgments of peer review panels often appear to be greatly influenced by one or two powerful (and, therefore, automatically persuasive) members of the panel—"esteemed practitioners"—usually with high rank and prestigious credentials.

Panels are often not panels at all but a grouping of eminent people with related subspecialties. Particular areas that come up for judgment are passed down to the subspecialist, making that person, in effect, a panel of one. Studies of panels also show they usually go along with the "resident experts," often charismatic people who have a high impact on their peers.

Peers and panelists are sometimes quick to "climb on the bandwagon." Going along with the current established scientific tide makes them more confident about their judgments and less vulnerable to second-guessers.

Thirdly, accomplishing a research goal or objective does not necessarily mean there has been a successful research effort. Maybe it took too long; maybe it was far too expensive for what was needed; and perhaps the research did not matter in the first place. On the other hand, the researcher occasionally makes a breakthrough—sometimes not even in the area of inquiry by simply hitting it lucky.

Not accomplishing a research goal doesn't necessarily mean the effort was unsuccessful. The real test is (1) whether the research effort went through a gauntlet of controlled administrative mechanisms that (2) minimized the risk at (3) every step of a long haul. This should be management's honest criteria. For example, we have discovered no basic cure or underlying fundamental medical reason why so many people get cancer. Are we to say, then, that cancer-related research efforts have been a failure? Not at all.

If our major assumptions are correct, it becomes reasonable to conclude that the least number of organizational gambles results in the best research effort; conversely, the best effort is based on a process in which the organization has taken the least chances. The laws of probability predict that this organization will have, more often than not, the highest number of possible successes.

The question must be asked, was each and every research effort carried out under the best administrative control and in response to well-thought-out goals of action—step by step, expenditure by resource expenditure? If so, each managerial project was a success, and each manager did the best he could up to this point. Continuing this effort should result finally in practical solutions or at least the best odds for success.

We can conclude that the process itself should be the major criterion in measuring past research efforts or in the administrative evaluation of the proposals for research funding. The "advertising" syndrome—"my expert says this is a good investigative approach, what does your expert say?" or "my expert says go; and when my expert talks, everybody should listen"—can be very unproductive.

What, then, is an acceptable management assessment process? How can auditors, evaluators, managers, or other people with good sense monitor and evaluate in a reliable and useful way the research process itself? Questions like the following can provide meaningful answers:

1. How did the first administrative decision to go ahead and establish research objectives come about?
2. Was there a proper advance blending of financial resources, organizational research policy, and determination of available technical resources?

3. Were all available data banks, in- or out-of-house, satisfactorily searched?
4. Was the literature in related matters fully scanned to see whether all or part of the studies proposed were previously attempted and whether they were successful or failures (and why) in part or in full?

Many of the so-called coincidental recordings of similar and even precisely duplcative research results (and dead-end costly efforts) could have been avoided by adequate data bank scrutiny. Researchers naturally push ahead when they are enthusiastic about a line of inquiry. They often do not know about previous failures in the same area, nor do they want to be dissuaded from relying on parallel lines of inquiry. They want to be the first there!

5. What were the bases for doing all or part of the research in- or out-of-house?
6. Who decided these things?
7. What facts dictated the answer?
8. Were sufficient cost-benefit studies made to test the contracting decisions?

Obviously, assessment must be made of the end product as well as of the documentation of the research process and the strategy for discovery. End product assessment is very often an important missing link tying the past to the future through an *auditable data bank.*

These questions illustrate the principal lines of audit inquiry. The inquiry should enable any evaluator to determine whether the organization did the best it could to maximize its chances of doing successful research at minimum cost.

None of this is new. It is part of the old, familiar "decision tree" methodology—program evaluation and review techniques, zero-based budgeting, and so forth—used in many management processes. An ancillary "decision-branch" analysis of each limb is also part of this process. The analytic technique is combinative. The entire evaluation process entails possibilities that multiply geometrically. It can, however, be handled in a practical manner through step-by-step monitoring and inquiries based on common sense.

More descriptive detail to fully develop these thoughts is probably not needed since this type of audit or evaluative procedure is fairly routine. The important point is that the step-by-step combination enables useful assessments, no matter how esoteric the research subject.

Many candid and perceptive scientists have told me that if a researcher cannot explain to an intelligent high school student what is going on and how it is being done, the researcher probably does not understand his or her subject that well—and in all likelihood is just fishing around.

Furthermore, research fraud has currently added a whole new dimension of powerful motivations that causes audit concern. As sad as it may seem, an increasing number of cases have been reported of fraudulent research—principally, claims made for research that was never done or done with different results. Identifying such practices is admittedly tricky, but possible. These audit reviews are easier when current and on-line. Auditing basic research is a hard challenge that should be considered by competent and sophisticated auditors.

POINT SHEET

The No-Product Dilemma

Auditors Rarely Engage in Assessing Basic Research	A serious void results; the stakes are high.
	Auditors can perform well in this area.
Three Basic Assumptions	(1) All research is a gamble; basic research is the riskiest.

(2) Going ahead merely on the reliance of "expert peers" is not fully satisfactory.

Peers have personal biases.

The are unduly influenced by powerful members.

Panels of peers usually consist of a grouping of specialists.

(3) Accomplishing a research goal does not necessarily connote success if it

Took too long.

Was too expensive.

Had trivial results.

Not accomplishing a goal is not necessarily bad.

Real Criteria for Research Success Is Nature of Controlled Process

Auditor should see

Whether proper administrative decisions were taken.

If advance blending of finances and know how was done.

If data banks were searched.

If the literature was scoured.

If in- or out-of-house decisions were valid.

Whether the potential principal researcher could explain his or her objective.

14

Fraud, The Ugly Spectre

When an auditor is actively on the lookout for fraud, his or her horizons will become endless. Deceit and trickery, leading to an illegal deprivation of property or rights—where cannot one find them nowadays even if one looks with half-closed eyes?

EVERYDAY EXAMPLES

Let's take the first factor in the definition of fraud—deceit—and relate it to a simple everyday encounter. Examine any large neighborhood supermarket and in all likelihood you will find clear-cut evidence of fairly widespread deceitful practices.

The cheese section: Over a period of time, the plastic wrap on certain types of cheeses can begin to bulge and become distorted, owing to the presence of gas created by bacilli that thrive in less-than-air-tight packages. It is not necessarily harmful, and it usually won't make you sick. But I'm sure that given the option, most customers would prefer to buy cheese in tightly sealed packets with no evident expansion. For one thing, it tastes better.

Deceit enters the picture because store personnel will, more often than not, make special efforts to put this less desirable merchandise right up in the front of the cheese section. They hope that a hurried customer, without looking closely, will select and drop one into his shopping cart. One could facetiously dub this as the BIOT principle (Bad Items On Top). Supermarket policy is nevertheless assuredly against this practice. But I have tested this situation many times over by slyly putting the bloated packet in the back of the cheese grouping and then upon returning in 30 minutes or so, finding it, once again, up front.

Why is it that meats always seem less pinkish at the check-out counters than they do at meat counter? Many supermarket chains have a dark red wallpaper design behind the cold meat bins. The wallpaper reflects the regular fluorescent white bulb light from the red background onto the meats, making them look artificially rosier. Another technique is to have slightly pinkish fluorescent bulbs over the entire meat section. It's legal—but is it deceitful or just good sales practice? Almost all items of produce are always arranged with their best side up so that blemishes and spoiled areas are hidden. Deceitful? Absolutely. Fraudulent? Certainly, since by definition, deceit is fraud. The practice is not criminal, however, and civil damages could easily be obtained. Stores will give you a replacement item. Is there intent to deceive? Of course, how can they deny it?

At the check-out counters, many large orders contain at least one error on the cash register, according to a recent study. In over 90 percent of the instances, the error was in favor of the store. The errors are usually not overtly fraudulent actions by the check-out clerk. But they are wrong in a sufficient number of instances to offset the unbiased rules of chance. What was probably occurring in many cases was a combination of two factors. One was the clerk's fear of being caught by the management ringing up items under the ticket price. So when the clerk was in doubt, he automatically used the higher price. The second is probably subliminal. He wanted the company to do well so as to better protect his job. Therefore, the slips of the fingers were almost all on the side of the store.

Let us leave the thousands of supermarkets and proceed to the restaurant, tavern, and fast food business. Who knows how many of them are out there. Here, too, there are almost endless techniques employed for deceiving customers.

Frozen ingredients are used while menus will claim them to be fresh (fresh as opposed to spoiled?). Prepackaged, commercial ingredients are substituted for so-called "scratch" items; lower-graded liquors than expected, or asked for, are used in mixed drinks prepared out of sight of the customers by the bartender; reconstituted, ground-up meats or seafood are used in lieu of the real items ("pork chopette"), and on.

COMMON EXAMPLES OF TRICKERY

Are all these just sharp sales techniques, or do they point towards trickery, the second element or fraud? Advertising deceitfulness is so widespread and ingenious as to be an international art form. Granted much of it is just sales puffery, and should be easily recognizable by the public, but an awful lot of it is downright deceitful and blatantly intended to deprive you of your property (money). Merchandisers want you to pay more or to buy their product, because it is 27 percent stronger, significantly sudsier, longer lasting, or tastier. Twenty-seven percent stronger than what? Tastier by whose standard? The point is that the public is being deliberately misled or deceived.

How about new and used cars. Is there any person reading this book that can honestly say that he never paid for or never heard of someone who paid for car service that was not performed or not performed as specified?

COMBATING THE PROBLEM

In retail establishments, shoplifting has reached incredible levels. Electronic door devices, loop wires, cabinet locks, and plastic snares are visible everywhere merchandise is sold. There are also one-way mirrors, peepholes, and undercover detectives. Total loss estimates are hard to come by because department stores and others are reluctant to let customers know just how much indirect costs are added to individual retail sales stickers to offset the overall massive shoplifting losses.

FRAUD WITHIN THE GOVERNMENT SECTOR

Take government-related operations—welfare, social security, Medicaid, medical providers, nursing homes, laboratories, and so on. One has to admit to never having read a newspaper or magazine recently or watched certain television shows not to have learned of the widespread abuses reported and testified to by various chief auditors in federal programs and by authorities involved in all the state and local entities. Recipients of public assistance, for instance, have been found to be receiving the same cash benefits from several localities at the same time. Vendors have made billings for services never rendered.

Cheating on federal and state tax forms, at least in a mild form, is a national hobby practiced quite artfully by many individual taxpayers. Active searching for any tax advantage, however wispy or vague, is also fair game in the eyes of sophisticated corporate lawyers and tax wizards. They know that (at its worst) "creative" tax preparation, in favor of their clients, is a good gamble. Credit card counterfeiting and corporate espionage add to the list in a significant way.

AN ANALYSIS OF THE SITUATION

I have presented this negative litany of baser characteristics to try to impress upon the reader that audits of almost any business, large or small, governmental or private, will encounter the strong possibility of fraud—deceit, trickery, or deprivation of property.

It will require the very best techniques and judgment the auditor can provide, in all of his engagements, to sort out whether the potential or reality of fraud is present, and, much harder, whether the reality is material and significant or merely trivial. If indicators of fraud are present, does it appear to be common practice; that is, are most employees involved?

Add to all of this the concern that the hardest-to-uncover frauds may be collusive and/or computer based, with very sophisticated and ingenious subterfuge. These are the cases where operations and records are so numerous and widespread that the auditor must be both a supertechnician and a truly rounded Renaissance man to be able to even understand and cope with the varieties and subtleties of all the possible situations he may encounter.

Here are some additional sobering facts. In 1978, the/Inspector/General for the then Department of HEW, estimated, in his annual report to the public and the Congress, that fraud and abuse in programs funded by his department alone could likely total $8 billion. All agree that it was a ball park figure that included waste, but it had enough documented support and circumstantial evidence to make it a very sobering disclosure. Add to this the potential for abuse and deceit in all the other federal departments, in hundreds of major state agencies, in thousands of cities and counties, tens of thousands of small and major corporations, and millions of individuals. One must admit that there exists an almost unlimited universe for fraud all waiting for the auditor as he enters the business arena. His graduation briefcase, by now burnished with a comfortable patina on the handle, and worn a little around the edges, is just not enough of a shield.

You the auditor may feel defenseless entering this well-documented jungle of fraud and greed, but you need not be. Your professional skills can be sharpened to a degree by which you can achieve realization of the AICPA's standards calling for due professional care.

The auditor can and must help. But what are the auditor's responsibilities—to his client, to the public at large, and to his own conscience? Are they different in each case? Also, what do the standards of the profession call for? What do the clients and the public at large expect? Probably more than the average auditor is now equipped to deliver—despite the requirements set forth in the professional standards.

The answers to these basic questions are not simple because the questions are so basic, and the more basic a subject is, the harder it is to definitively explain it.

Of course, understanding all the various motives behind each of the millions of frauds committed each year is obviously impossible. Illicit gain is not the only factor. Social attitudes that push people to acquire unjust gains or avoid uncovered defects or troubles are very tough to understand. While we cannot understand all of the motives, we do know how to uncover fraudulent situations and to protect ourselves against them.

Let us, now, relate our discussion to the auditor's professional responsibilities. Clients, such as small businesspeople, generally expect their auditors to protect them from practically all potential defrauders of any consequence. The client expects to be helped by the installation of a good tight accounting system, and physical-asset internal control mechanisms so that the chances for stealing from him are minimized.

If, however, despite all these controls, through collusion or other adept means, the business is defrauded, I think the client will accept it as something that could happen to anyone, and he is likely to be tolerant of the situation, but only if—and this is a big if—his own auditor found the defalcation or abuse himself and in time to prevent very material losses.

When a large business is defrauded, the client primarily expects his own personnel or his intrinsic internal monitoring system to bring to the surface aberrant or abusive operations. For example, a large department store would not expect its CPA firm to find and stop shoplifters or discover cashier malfeasance, but a small neighborhood store owner would. He (or she) expects his much more closely related CPA to tell him if he suspected cheating sales employees or cashier abuse.

Everybody expects much more from auditors in this entire arena that the average journeyman can now deliver. Many auditors just are not equipped to respond to the challenge. Why not? Inadequate training at the university level is cited by most perceptive audit managers. Why so? If I had to cite one reason only, I think I would pick the fact that we mistakenly assume that graduate *accountants* are educationally equipped *auditors*. Not so. Examine the table of contents of this book. Are many of these subjects taught to most of the students graduating nowadays who will be seeking jobs with auditing firms? At the very least, I suggest that auditors make themselves aware of what kind of training is needed and pursue it.

SOURCES OF TEMPTATION

Just to demonstrate the possibilities, let me list and outline a number of possible subjects for abuse. The points that I make here can be used for small and medium-sized businesses or refined and modified for giant concerns. This is merely intended to illustrate the point and just to stimulate your "thinking" on the subject. It is obviously, by no means, definitive, but is designed merely to be a helpful "memory jogger" for the auditor and is subdivided for reference purposes only.

Cash (The Most Worrisome Asset)

1. Are receipts and disbursements functions separated? Watch out for the employee who handles both of these.
2. Is there a disbursing document for every payable?
3. Petty cash—if not so petty, why is it so big? Who needs all that cash?
4. Who signs the checks and on what authority? Why isn't a checkwriter employed? Where is the blank checkbook? (People can steal blank checks from the book, cash them in, and be discovered too late to be easily caught.)
5. Cash records should be absolutely current; receipts should be deposited and recorded as fast as possible. If

they aren't, be wary. Everything a business does should be timely and on-line. This rule is material in reducing the possibility of fraud.

6. Remember that current bank reconciliations (and cut-off disbursement checks) are mandatory. Any delay in this process, or discouragement about outside cut-off techniques, is a very bad vibe!

7. Remember, too, that strict physical control over cash helps to preclude potentially abusive situations. Also, do not condone any arguments for having accounts of cash on hand that are in excess of current needs. It's 99.4 percent faulty.

8. Excess cash even in checking accounts is also a hazardous company policy. Ask yourself, Why is it necessary? If nothing else, possible interest is lost.

9. Add up cash register tapes once in a while. I have found them to be open to manipulation, despite assertions to the contrary. Don't ask me how—I don't know. But they can be altered, and it doesn't take a person with a "computer-wizard" mind to do it.

10. Lastly, with respect to cash in retail businesses, the underlying concept, as far as auditors are concerned, is to see how it ties in directly to individual sales. If you were to ask me to pick out one device more useful than any others, it would be prenumbered sales slips (fully accounted for, in advance of use).

Receivables

It goes without saying that receivables are far more worrisome than payables. Obviously, the entity's suppliers, that is, those businesses owed money, will let you know if the organization makes errors, deliberate or otherwise, in their accounts.

11. Therefore, the key thing to look for in the receivable area is how good is the direct tie-in to the *source* of the receivables. What did the company give up or sell to create an obligation on the part of someone else? How does the accounting system keep track of the substitution of one asset for another? For example, suppose the business is a car repair shop. It could be called a swap shop because it swaps its mechanics' time and the replacement/repair parts it owns in return for cash or a payment by credit card.

The auditor, of course, should devise checks to see that the swap is equitable and in keeping with service repair sales policy. (Is the swap equitable? could be a very good general rule of thumb.) The value of an hour of the mechanics' time should be revealed by comparing the appropriateness of charges to customers with payables for spare parts purchases, to residual inventories. All have a direct relationship to billing tickets.

One good example of an overall check might be to add up one whole week's transactions and see how the sum compares to the total payroll and spare parts charges, including the special purchases made in a given week for the specific needs of certain cars.

Payrolls

Payrolls is an area fraught with potential fraud and abuse. A number of sample questions should be answered and should trigger many more. The size and nature of the business operation will naturally affect your responses.

12. Who gets on the payroll and by whose approval?
13. How are changes in pay to individuals authorized?
14. Who controls the basic personnel records?
15. How are payroll checks prepared, or if the payroll is in cash, who calculates the totals and the specifics?

16. If the payroll system is computerized, many more problems are possible. Who prepares the computer programming and has access to the hardware (and software)?
17. What about deductions from net pay—bonds, taxes, insurance, contributions and dues, company loans, and so forth? The totals in these referenced accounts should be tied in, periodically, with the payroll totals (and with personnel "action" records).
18. Are Social Security numbers bona fide? You would be surprised by how many are not.
19. If the auditee is a large, impersonal organization, are floor checks routinely made, at least on a sample basis?

Inventories

20. Count them on time during the entire year on a controlled cyclical basis.
21. Study them. Are they representative of present-day company sales or production? (Expensive, outmoded, unneeded inventories are not worth what the books say they are.)
22. Are the inventories portable or easily hidden and expensive? If so, be alert to fraud (and, of course, theft).
23. Remember always that receivables and inventories can be converted to cash, which is eminently "stealable," especially when hidden by computerized recordkeeping.

POINT SHEET

FRAUD, THE UGLY SPECTRE

It Is Sickenly Prevalent	Fraud is everywhere. Everyday, supermarkets employ sharp business practices, or perhaps

more. There are examples in the text to alert the reader.

Nuisance "frauds" are practiced by restaurants and like businesses; you simply don't get what you pay for.

The advertising game is another case where you don't get what you pay for

Common business tactics combat another type of fraud—theft. All consumers pay for stolen business property through higher prices.

Cheating the government is widely practiced.

Disreputable people rip off their own government through various scams.

An Analysis of the Situation

The auditor must face up to his or her responsibilities.

They are plentiful.

Meeting these responsibilities appears tough, but the answer to the question how is so basic that it is difficult to adequately and definitively explain.

Be aware that smaller clients expect much more in the way of fraud deterrence from the auditor than do larger clients.

What Can the Auditor Do to Prepare for the Fight?

Education, at the very least.

Memory Joggers

Sensitive areas in any business.

Cash (most worrisome).

Receivables (the key step: tying in the source of the receivables to "benefits" accruing.

Payrolls (fraught with potential fraud and abuse).

Inventories (Count them. Compare them to records).

PART FIVE

Summation: Comparing What Was to What Should Have Been

To many auditors the toughest part of an assignment is the summation. You and I, though, and perhaps a few others have never dreaded this task. In fact, we rather enjoy it. Why? Simple, really—it's one of the most interesting mental exercises around. An audit report, particularly one covering internal audit assignments challenges you to (1) consider the meaning, impact, and relatability of the many conditions that surface during any audit, and (2) sort these observations into an understandable set of findings and then pull this material into a package that will "sell" your views to the ultimate reader.

Here are a few basic insights that I have gathered and developed over the years that can be used to pull together a salable audit report—or for that matter any written or oral communication.

First, keep simplicity of presentation as one of your top objectives. Your audience should never need to ponder over your report since this causes points to be missed, or perhaps worse, misunderstanding. Personally, I become annoyed at having to interpret what someone has written for me (or is trying to tell me). Take pity on your audience by carefully structuring your presentation in such a manner that it can be understood without too much struggle. To me, this means that up front, you discuss what you are going to say. Amplify your remarks to include such needed detail as impact, scope, presumed importance of the subject, and the like. (This is your overview section, of course.) The AICPA Standards explicitly instruct the auditor, "Do not deceive the reader."

Next, as you discuss details, always fit them into a framework that is readily apparent to your reader. A simplistic example would be a report to a landlord.

"This problem concerns a house located at 111 Park Street."

Now as for what's wrong with the house:

"The plumbing is in need of repair."

More specific details now follow.

"Its tenants are threatening to sue you as the landlord unless prompt repairs are made." Your reader's attention is now riveted on the problem, but more details are needed. Need I go on?

Last, it is sometimes helpful to restate, in general terms, the highlights of what has just been said. This leaves your audience with no doubt as to the points that you wish to make. You are doing them a favor by refreshing their memories with pertinent facts and are doing yourself the favor of making sure that the impact of what you have just related has not been lost. But make sure that the restatement fits the original thoughts.

The auditing community does have a number of prescribed formats and methods of presentation for reporting on the results of its work. Following these formal guides, together with the more easygoing guidance given in this section, will enable the practitioner to develop and produce a professional product.

15

The "How To" of Writing an Audit Finding

It has been said that "in public or private life, the effective man is the man who can think clearly, say what he means, and put his ideas across on paper. He can clear out verbal brier patches, straighten sentences that have gone awry, and shorten the "distance" from the page to the eyes. His credo is basically Thoreauvian: Simplify, simplify.

But the art of effective and simple communication is not a magic affair that should be delegated to writing magicians. Every person who has to write any kind of report must accept this responsibility himself.

All auditors have an intrinsic responsibility to report on, or more exactly, give a precise presentation of the facts of his or her investigation. Individual findings must stand on their own merit and be reported as self-standing descriptions and narrations.

There are a number of ways to simplify the reporting of audits and the presentation of findings. One might begin by showing (1) what well-developed audit findings have in common, regardless of subject matter. (2) how weaknesses in findings can be identified, (3) how this information can be utilized in writing and further developing findings, and (4) helpful hints for applying this knowledge. The individual attributes of audit findings—how they can be identified and used—will be discussed later. The questions now arise, How do we judge an entire finding, and how can we take advantage of its basic attributes in actually writing better findings and summaries and any other self-contained portion of an audit report?

What are the basic concepts or common denominators? Let me back up a little bit and discuss the elements of any good nonfictional writing. If you were to ask 10 experts how to go about becoming a better writer, you would surely get 10 entirely different answers and methodologies.

But what are some of the basic points that all these experts and many others make in one form or another? They all say that you must:

Organize your thoughts.

Outline your thoughts.

Find the words and sentence structure to convey your thoughts in a concise, grammatical, and persuasive manner.

Practice using these techniques.

Read and study other writer's material.

These points indicate that good, effective findings and report writing (and for that matter, any writing) require a lot of study, practice, analysis, and hard work. You cannot sell a product unless you package it well, but even if you package it attractively, only good contents get repeat orders. Trite but true! Audit packages (reports) are no different.

This section discusses findings in general, their strengths and weaknesses, and elaborates on the first two steps above: (1) organization of thoughts, and (2) outlining of main points. It seems clear, however, that these two steps cannot be successfully taken before you make sure that your analysis of a particular finding indicates that it has a valid point of view a reader can clearly understand. This thought process is really not much different from the generation of an informed opinion on any subject. Is the situation you are describing good, bad, or something in between, and on what do you base your opinion?

So-called good management concepts are really nothing more than a composite of previously established authoritative criteria in any particular business area. Do you rely on them for what you are trying to tell the reader in the finding? What is your overall opinion or point of view? It is unfair and unreliable to have the reader sort out your facts, decide on their relative importance, and conclude what they really mean. That's the job of the auditor who was on the scene.

STRUCTURING THE FINDING

When you have decided whether the situation is good or bad and have substantiated reasons for this decision, the remaining task is to put your thoughts on paper. Put the main point down first, then edit and subdivide the main point if necessary. Show what documentation or statistics you have to prove the point of illustration and what harm, if any, the situation results in. Use the underlying cause as a recommendation for a cure. Of course, all this presupposes that you have done the basic audit work to authenticate an intelligent and useful opinion.

Once you have been able to do this, the rest is a matter of writing tight, semantically attractive sentences, using interesting, active words, spelling them correctly, having them typed neatly, editing the results, and seeing to it that they make good sense. Do all this and you should end up with a clear, and interesting report—provided, once again, that you started with a good examination or audit and one that fully supports your point of view. It should not be surprising to find that those who successfully recognize all the needed attributes of the end product report to begin with (before the audit) usually perform a superior field audit afterwards.

In any event, the schematic description in Figure 1 and the supplementary notes provide helpful "how to" comments regarding findings and the way one actually goes about writing them.

Major Theme

The first paragraph (or two or three, if necessary) represents a summary of the auditor's overall point of view. He (or she) has to decide what he is trying to say about this particular finding and what his composite evaluation is. The first paragraphs of a finding should have the same relation to the rest of the finding that a summary has to the remainder of a report containing a number of findings. One could express it mathematically in this very simple fashion:

The first paragraph:		(is to the)
Rest of the finding	=	(as the)
Summary of the report:		(is to the)
Entire Report		

The first paragraph really sets the tone for what follows and serves to give the reader a quick synopsis of the finding, including the recommendation. It should therefore include the five attributes common to all good writing. It is interesting to note that you can usually tell, almost in direct relation to the difficulty you experience in writing the summary paragraph, the number of missing attributes in the whole finding.

Each finding should be self-sustaining and the reader should not have to depend on what was said in previous findings (or subsequent ones) to fully understand the present one. The major theme, in effect, tells the reader to expect explanatory narrative that will support and explain the basis for the overall point of view. The order in which you describe this in the summary paragraph should be the same order in which you later elaborate on them in the body of the finding. It is important to give the reader a sense of tempo, perspective, and orderly sequence, right from the outset.

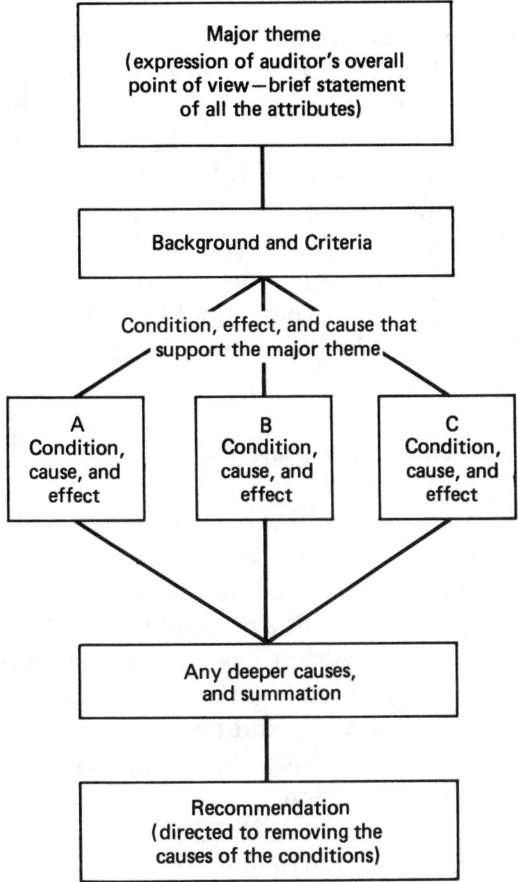

Figure 1. Schematic description of a typical finding.

Background and Criteria

After you have given the reader your overall point of view and he (or she) can generally picture the entire finding, provide a sense of balance by stepping back a few paces. Discuss the background of the situation and whatever criteria you are measuring the management performance against. This tends to give the narration perspective and indicates what set of values are being considered in this particular situation.

As previously stated, many criteria can be used—stipulated policies, excerpts from the law, citations of good management procedures, or even in certain cases, your own expert opinion. This last criterion should be used judiciously and should have some corroborative support in other forms, if possible. Here again, this paragraph, or paragraphs, should be fairly short. This is not to say, however, that when the whole finding hinges on the background and criteria, that you cannot expound on these to some length. But generally they should be fairly terse, allowing the reader to quickly slip from your major theme to the audit observations.

Description of Condition, Effect, and Cause

This is the section of the finding that tells what you found wrong. (or in some special cases what you find particularly right or well done), what effect it has had, and what caused the specific conditions. The continuity of thought, most report writers find, is enhanced if the section is generally arranged in this order—condition, effect, and cause. Usually this is where you narrate the main thrust of your finding, where you describe what you found, what harmful effects have resulted (or may result), and what caused the situation.

It may be necessary to have different subsections describing different elements of the particular finding; that is, accounting records, administrative controls, and procedures, and the availability of qualified personnel to carry these out. Perhaps program objectives were not being accomplished because resources were expended in the wrong problem area and management was not alerted. The issues may concern money expended needlessly or inappropriately; other resources may have been unnecessarily dissipated or used with only partial effectiveness. Any number of variables can exist.

All the subsections, however, must be related to your overall point of view and be part of the major theme. In each of the subsections it is likely that entire modules of related conditions will come into focus but the basic attributes still remain—condition, effect, and cause; and the analysis of these should be clearly visible.

In this part of the discussion, whole new sets of technical considerations and accounting standards also come into play—sampling techniques (or substitute judgmental analyses, if necessary), physical observations (i.e., inventorying), cost analyses, or even deductive reasoning if that is pertinent and reasonable under the circumstances. One central caution in this area (and this relates primarily to effect) is "Don't overreach." Exercise caution so that you do not create an issue larger than the facts actually warrant.

The sensitive and usually highly judgmental area of cause requires the most penetrating efforts and insights the auditor can call upon. It follows that readers find this to be the most consistently short-changed aspect of the entire evaluation and reporting task. As a minimum effort, the auditor should have dug into the situation deeply enough so that he can generate what we might term a "first level of recommendation," that is, one that is sufficiently detailed or specific enough to enable the recipient of the finding to correct, at the first or working level of management, the correctable conditions cited in the section. The following abstract of a recent letter from a program official to an auditor illustrates quite clearly the importance of cause to a competent report reader:

> *. . . Your audit has clearly defined several areas of major deficiency at various management levels, in implementing and managing the program during fiscal years 19XX and 19XX, resulting in dilution of the program's intended educational effect. In considering the alternative courses of remedial action available to us, we would benefit greatly from your specific assessment of the ultimate cause of each major deficiency set forth in your report.*
>
> *As one example, the draft report cites the lack of effective detailed analysis of project proposals prior to approval thereof and a lack of continuing meaningful surveillance, by management, of expenditures during operation of the approved projects. Please tell us whether in your view, those deficiencies stemmed, for instance, from insufficient staff availability (within or beyond our power to augment), lack of appropriate concern and diligence on the part of the organization, inadequacies of state policies or standard practices, misinterpretation or misunderstanding of the letter and spirit of*

the federal statute, regulations or guidelines, or inexperience or unawareness of key personnel.

Deeper Causes and Summation

This section is usually the easiest place to analyze the basic causes of the situation. It is also an easy place to overreach. However, in most cases it is very difficult to discuss the deeper causes or the philosophic reasons in a single finding or for that matter in a single audit report. Ordinarily—at least in the audit of a large organization—these can be adequately discussed only in a consolidated report of wide range and scope.

Nevertheless, it is a good place for a summation if you have many subdivisions in the finding. The summation should be very brief and serve only to bring the reader back to your major theme and to recapitulate your point of view. The summation is fairly easy to handle; the main danger is being overrepetitive. The approach can best be illustrated by an adage heard in the military services whenever an officer is to speak before an audience:

> Give them a road map.
>
> Tell them where you are going.
>
> Tell them what you want to tell them.
>
> After you tell them, then tell them what it was that you told them.

Recommendation

As previously mentioned, the recommendation will mostly be geared to the working level of management, where specific action can be taken. The recommendations should in all instances be identifiable with the main points in the findings and should, wherever possible, reflect practical solutions to the situations that need improvement or correction.

PUTTING IT DOWN ON PAPER

We have discussed the structure of a finding and its attributes. It may also be useful to talk briefly about the actual mechanics of getting your thoughts on paper. How do you get started?

Many good writers have described their techniques in this time sequence:

1. Jot down cryptic references to all the "bits and pieces" that you want to include in this finding. These shorthand notes serve as useful reminders for including all the subpoints of your finding.
2. After you jot down everything you can think of that may be pertinent to a given finding, decide what your main point of view is. This is a very important step. If you proceed without this overall analysis, you are inviting disjointed narration. One good way to test your point of view is by attempting to write the opening paragraph (major theme) and actually to construct the sentences that describe your evaluation. This effort gives you a quick check as to whether your overall point of view is clearly formed in your mind. If it does not come off smoothly, it is a good bet that more brainstorming is needed.
3. Build the rest of the finding step by step from your bits and pieces and see if they fit into a cohesive pattern, as described above. You can actually frame your finding in a short topic sentence for each of the areas and outline notes under each of the subheadings. It is generally conceded by the writing fraternity that it is quicker, simpler, and more effective in the long run to fully plan and outline your finding (or report) in advance and then to find the words and sentences that will clearly express your views. It is more likely that the findings will then have cohesion and will reflect a tempo of words and ideas that will enable the reader to easily follow your trend of thought.

4. Afterwards, read over what you have written, preferably after it has been typed. This permits a cold, composite (and, it is hoped, dispassionate) opinion of the whole finding.
5. Edit or rewrite if necessary. Scrap the finding, in part or in whole, if it has to be done. Above all, don't become enamored of your own efforts! Not many pieces of writing are perfect.

POINT SHEET

How to Write an Audit Finding

To Be Effective, Think Clearly Say What You Mean Put It on Paper	Effective communication is not a magic affair to be left to a writing magician. It is every auditor's responsibility to write his or her own report. Findings ought to be a form of self-contained report.
What Is the Technique? Experts Agree that Good Writers	Organize thoughts. Decide on overall theme. Outline thoughts. Then, find the words and sentence structure to convey evaluations concisely and persuasively. Practice, practice, practice. Read and study other writers' materials.
Saying This Differently	Decide on your overall point of view; this is your report—don't ask the reader to determine the relative importance of your points. Set the stage (background) and cite the criteria or value (what do you base your findings on—stipulated pol-

icies, law, good management principles, expert opinion).

Describe what was wrong (or particularly right).

Subdivide the main point, if necessary.

What was the total effect? Be careful at this point not to overreach; don't create an issue larger than the facts warrant.

Cause—this sensitive and usually highly judgmental area requires the most penetrating efforts and insights the auditor can call on (this topic is often short-changed).

Deeper causes and a summation may need a full report of wider range and scope than a single finding; here again, don't overreach.

Recommendations must be identifiable with the main point in your finding and reflect practical solutions for needed improvement.

Putting It Down on Paper (How to get Started in Five Easy Steps)

Jot Down Cryptic References to All the "Bits and Pieces"	These shorthand notes are useful reminders.
Decide on Main Point of View	Again, most important, write the opening paragraph; if this stumps you, rethink it.
Outline the "Bits into a Cohesive Outline	The words and phrases will come easier if this is done *first.*
Read over the Draft	After it is typed, give it a dispassionate appraisal.
Edit Rewrite and Scrap It All If Necessary	Above all, don't become enamored of your own efforts; hardly any first writings are perfect.

16

Summaries: The Bridge between Audit Effort and Detailed Disclosures

Summaries are considered effective when they successfully compare, in the shortest form possible, *what was* with *what should have been.* A short description should be included of the effect the findings had on programs or organizations, the root causes, and suggestions for related action.

I would like to illustrate how this comparing or balancing process works when related to summarizing the results of internal audits.

Four different types of summaries are frequently used:

1. The Comprehensive/Consolidated Report. This report analyzes underlying concepts, significant findings, and their trends in a series of independent subreports.
2. A Summary of a Single Report. This subreport is part of a comprehensive study but original in its own right.
3. The Summary Paragraph. One or two paragraphs summarize a single finding included in a report.

4. A Briefing Memo. The memo is intended to give the reader a quick synopsis of any of the above. It may also come from other sources, such as trip reports, personal observations, or special analyses.

1. THE COMPREHENSIVE REPORT

This type of report is used to consolidate and highlight broad, underlying factors inherent in a number of other reports. (Each of these other reports, of course, should already have been prepared with summaries. The writing of these summaries is discussed below under heading number 2.) In this document the main ingredient of success is the ability to synthesize the basic elements of managerial and administrative accomplishments that would have constituted good performance.

Comparing "what was" with "what should have been" is the key ingredient. When a writer begins a comprehensive report that summarizes a number of field subreports, he should be prepared, at the outset, to comment on all of the major points related to the scope of the examination covered by these separate reports. The managerial controls and administrative processes concerning these key functions either needed improvement (appropriate recommendations should be stated) or not (the audit disclosed no significant deficiencies). But he cannot be silent *on any of them* and consider the summary complete. There is, of course, no reason why he cannot subdivide any comments pertaining to these principal areas, if needed.

The Writing Process

It might be useful at this point to identify (in a general way) some of the steps in the organization of the subreport material and the thinking process associated with it.

1. Most important is the need for the writer to maintain his focus on what would constitute good performance. This

entire report has to be weighed against these initial and basic thoughts.

2. The next logical step is to summarize reported results by the main performance areas.

3. Decide on the total impact of these findings and how much of the total effort in each of the main areas was well done, or something less.

4. Reach a balance, based on demonstrated audit results, as to how well the entire organization performed in relation to what should have been done. Here again, if the audit does not disclose extreme or crystal clear results, a high degree of discretion has to be used in categorizing these results. I am referring to the "middle ground condition." With these it takes adroitness in finding the right words to express an opinion. It isn't always necessary, or desirable, to make flat out statements. Where exceptionally good or poor performance is evident, this may be justified. Here the natural conservativism of auditors is comfortably put aside in the case of these extremes. One could, for example, describe a nonextreme situation in these terms: "Our examination disclosed no significant problems in the procurement and inventory of goods and supplies." Or, "Other than the problems noted in the project approval process, we found no evidence of other administrative weakness."

5. It might also be necessary to trade off good and bad performance in each main functional area. Perhaps the organization did an excellent job in identification of needs, but did a very poor job in the evaluating and monitoring process. Despite the fact management was not looking over its own shoulder sufficiently to see that performance came out well, the end result may have still been very worthwhile; basic objectives may have been met (management will be delighted to read that although problems existed, the job was done.). One might then point out

that an effective monitoring process would help to insure good balanced performance in the future.

6. In describing what was accomplished well and what was not, it is essential to consider why things were not done well. The broader or deeper causes are often discernible or describable only in a comprehensive report. Many regard the full discussion of deep-set causes to be the primary function of this type of in-depth summation. Individual findings, or even entire subreports, often describe only localized superficial causes which may not relate to the broad scene.
7. Another major ingredient would be a discussion of the manner, or efficiency, of overall program operation. This should be considered in the mental balancing process already mentioned; for example, a program or project may have achieved a good part of the desired objectives despite gross inefficiencies in its administrative procedures. The point is that the money wasted in bad application of resources could be better allotted to other aspects of the program, or even to other programs. Uneconomical procurement, extraneous bookkeeping, and inadequate equipment or supplies control are every day examples. It is often useful to relate indirect, or nonprogram findings, to the main program or business objectives. (Did a lack of widgets delay production, for example.)
8. An opinion must also be offered (and it usually fits best in the scope) whether that which was audited was indeed representative of the whole. A report may still be sufficiently noteworthy in its own right, and of great interest to top management, even if it comments meaningfully only on certain aspects of the entire business.

The schematic in Figure 2 may help to illustrate graphically the entire process of writing a comprehensive report. It should be remembered, however, that the report "thinking" process should not be mistaken for the report "writing" procedure. The writing sequence differs from the developmental pattern. Before you draft the very first paragraph, think out the entire report. Then, start writing.

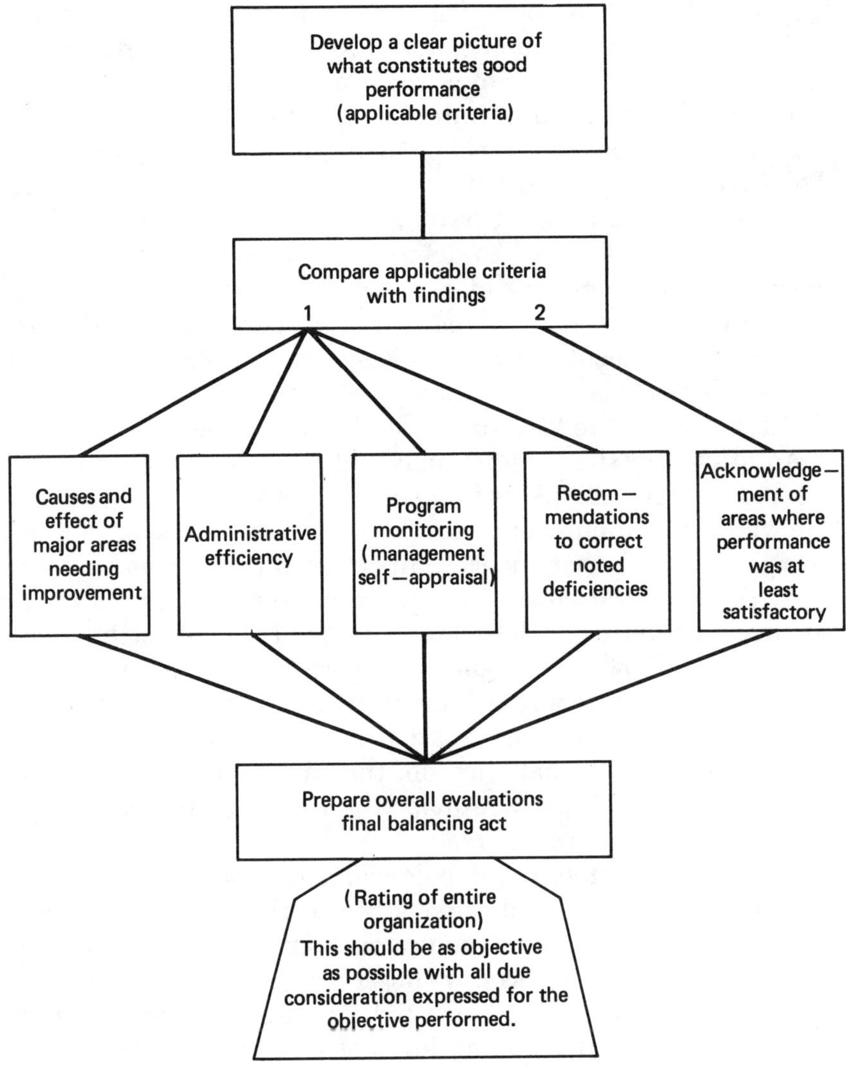

Figure 2. Description of the thought process involved in writing a comprehensive report summary.

2. SUMMARY OF A SINGLE REPORT (SUBREPORT TO A COMPREHENSIVE REPORT)

Many of the basic concepts involved in writing a comprehensive summary apply here, but with some important differences. For one, the scope is much more limited. Normally, it isn't possible to discuss, in depth, aspects of a whole program in only one report summary. But you can narrate how a broad program or project has worked in one state, a single plant, or even at one audit site. This type of report usually contains a number of findings designed to describe what went wrong. However, since findings are not usually designed to describe what went right, the main purpose of the summary of a report is to provide the balance needed to put adverse findings in proper perspective with positive accomplishments. One could easily visualize a report with a fair number of solid findings that might still show that the overall situation was well handled. The job was done!

Additionally, the findings may only be concerned with the need to correct weaknesses in relatively less important aspects of the whole operation. Here, too, the writer has to visualize in his or her own mind what the elements of good performance are and what the organization should have done to get high marks. The summary, therefore, is the proper area to discuss offsetting items and describe how the organization performed as a whole (presumably it did quite well if there were no findings). To reiterate, the audit effort must be adequate to support these statements. If it is less than clear that they do, the writer then must balance (that key word) what was done (the actual audit scope) with what he can report to the reader.

Avoid feeble attempts at balancing. All too frequently, one sees reports that give only lip service to the balancing process. For example, "The organization carried out its administrative responsibilities well. However, we observed a number of significant weaknesses that should be corrected. These are . . ." and so on. In my view, this is contradictory and not a good summary. It does not describe, at least in short form, what positive administrative functions were satisfactorily carried out. A description or analysis of these well-accomplished functions could be supplemented by describing what weak areas slipped by managerial control, and why. That could be the central theme of a report of this type.

Another ineffective type of summary is one that merely contains a consolidated grocery list of the report findings. It usually appears as a short paragraph summarizing each finding, and it frequently fails to give the reader a feel for the entire picture. At its worst, it appears as an almost word-for-word reproduction of the first paragraph of each finding, placed in the front of the report.

The third type of summary of a subreport that misses the target is one where there are no findings and the writer merely gives the organization a one- or two-sentence verbal pat on the back because of this. He does not let the reader know just what it was that earned the organization a good mark. What did it actually do well? How was it able to successfully handle the program objectives and administrative functions with which it was charged? It does not take much to describe this briefly. If the writer feels comfortable to sign off without any findings, he should certainly have enough knowledge to describe what was well done and how and have enough confidence in the audit process to say so.

The schematic in Figure 3 illustrates the comparison process involved in individual report summaries.

3. THE SUMMARY PARAGRAPH

Summarizing a single finding involves a process entirely different from summarizing comprehensive or individual reports. The basic difference is that the writer does not always have to provide a balance in the description of conditions that are not applicable to each particular finding.

The main purpose of the summary of a finding is to present in condensed form (1) the nature of the weakness, (2) the reason for these shortcomings, and (3) the extent of these shortcomings.

This gives the reader a quick idea of what went wrong, why it went wrong, and how wrong it was. Also, what needs to be done to correct things! The writer need not talk about all the other things that were correctly handled in the summary of a finding. That is the function of the full report summary relating to all the findings. Nevertheless, summing up the individual finding is a crucial task because this enables, and forces, the writer to determine what the condition is all about and gives the reader a chance to skip the details if he desires.

4. THE BRIEFING MEMO

This type of writing evokes an entirely new set of summary thoughts. A briefing memo is intended to capsule an entire situation, or an entire organization's performance, in as few words as possible. Conciseness is crucial. The reader, while not knowing the intimate details of what went right and what went wrong, should nevertheless be able to get a strong grasp of whether the overall situation is good or bad, and how good or bad it is. One or two very brief illustrations of the conditions are often very useful.

Good, tight briefing memos are deceptively difficult to write successfully. The writer must first, in his own mind, make all the judgments necessary for the reader to come up to a clear view of the situation. The reader has to immediately feel that he can rely on it, since he lacks knowledge of the intimate details of the situation being discussed. A briefing memo is not useful, or well written, if the reader feels queasy about the summary judgments.

CONCLUSION

In conclusion (and this illustrates a fifth type of summation) the summary is, by any criteria, the most critical element of all reports. It can and should be the focal point of communication between the writer and reader. If done well, the balanced insight

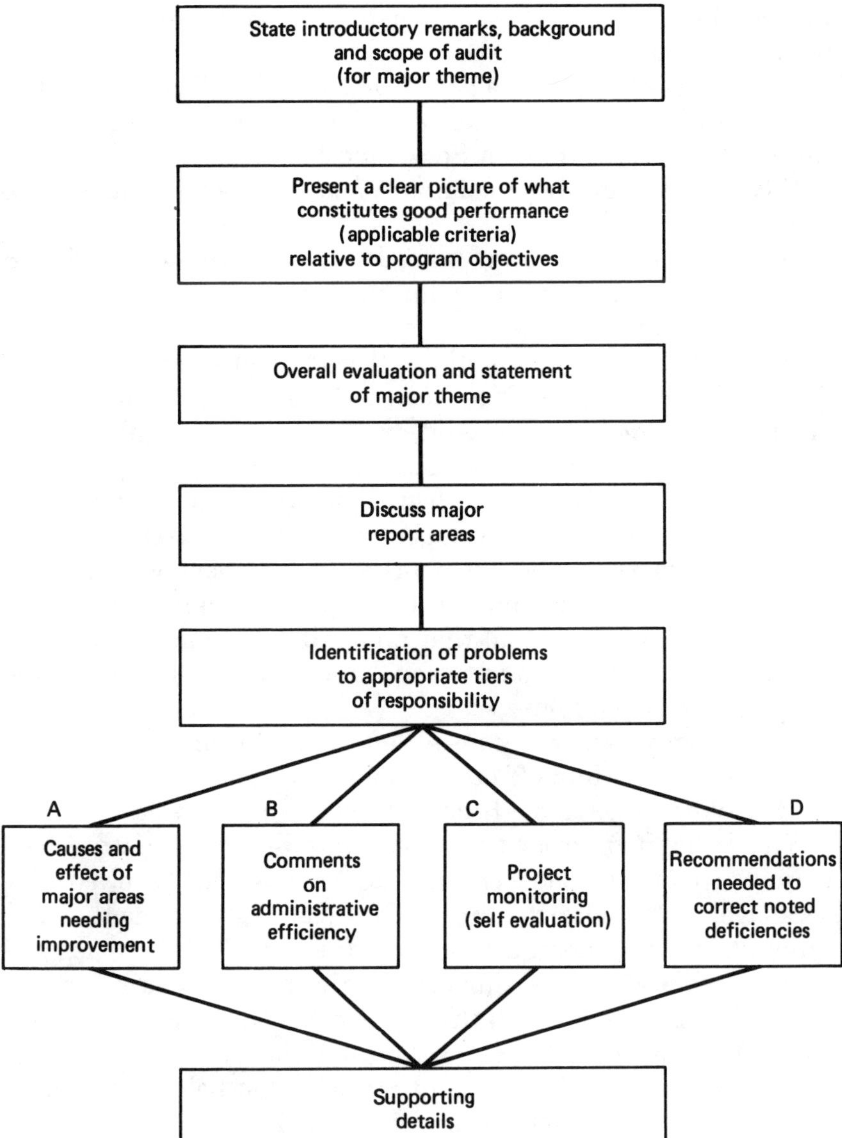

Figure 3. Summary of a single report.

will provide a quick and useful perspective on the supporting details and conditions observed.

I would like to present a short, probably familiar story, call it a fable, to illustrate the matter of "misplaced emphasis." Let's call it "Kropatkin's Law of Socks and Sassing."

Scene: Boy, (any boy) coming home from school, anxious to run out and play.

"Get back in here, young man; I want a word with you!"

"But Mom, Jim's waiting for me," the young boy whines. "Can't it wait?"

"Gregory," replies his mother, "I want you to straighten up, and straighten up fast. You have left your room a mess. How about your homework, eh? And, my friend, don't think I'm forgetting how you sassed your father last night when he told you to turn off the TV and go to bed. That was unforgivable."

Shaken by his mother's anger and suddenly contrite, Greg quickly apologizes. And his mother—as mothers will—quickly hugs her son and sends him on his way with a quick pat.

"Hey Greg, what was all that noise about? Sounded like your mother was chewing you out good," Jim asks as his friend comes running out of the house.

"Oh, Mom was mad because I left my socks under the bed . . . and I've been goofing off on my homework."

"My old man gave me heck last night, too. What a life."

This young man wasn't quite accurate in recapping this little episode. All of the facts were there, but just slightly skewed. The socks were left under the bed as Greg said. But the mother was upset about the general condition of the boy's bedroom, not just a few stray socks. Most important, the mother was infuriated about the manner in which the boy had talked to his father. This was left out in the retelling of the tale.

The moral here, of course, is that one must be ever conscious of the effect of a misplaced or missing emphasis in retelling an event—or summarizing a writing. The whole meaning can be changed or, as in this little example, missed altogether if one is not careful. This process must also be faithfully followed by those of us in the auditing profession.

You have done your work, made your findings, and painstakingly developed your recommendations. Your report is written, and, it is hoped, is a well-balanced presentation.

One major writing chore awaits—boiling it down for the busy, weary executive to read and comprehend. Your skill at distinguishing between "socks and sassing" can sell your professional opinions and observations. A poorly developed digest of even the best report can result in reader misunderstanding. Keep in mind that the report's digest may well be the only part of the report that will be read by the majority of its readers.

Sit back and consider carefully the points you wish to make. Rank their importance. See whether several minor points can be correlated into one single observation—sort those socks! Don't hesitate to stress points that you may believe are obvious. Others may not have your interpretive skills. Be careful, though, about the stress you place on issues of minor substance.

Coming back to Greg for a moment, and applying Kropatkin's Law: He sassed his dad (that's important!). He also didn't do his homework and left his room a mess! That's the way to report on this little episode, or any set of findings.

POINT SHEET

SUMMARIES: THE BRIDGE BETWEEN AUDIT EFFORT AND DETAILED DISCLOSURE

Compare "What Was" With "What Should Have Been." (Four Frequently Used Types)

Comprehensive/consolidated report—analyzes underlying concepts, significant findings, trends in a series of independent subreports.

Single report—a subreport, above, but original in its own right.

Summary of a finding

Briefing memo—quick synopsis of any of the above.

Curt executive note—like "Don't close the plant in Iowa."

Comprehensive Report (Key Ingredient of the Writing Process: A Comparison of "What Was" with "What Should Have Been")	Absolutely imperative to mentally decide what would have constituted good performance. Summarize main performance areas. Impact of findings? Exceptional performance easy (good or bad); "middle ground" needs most attention. Trade off good and bad areas. Consider why things were not done well—usually only deep comprehensive reports can do this. Consider efficiencies—things may have been done well, but at a prohibitive cost. Consider also—was that which was audited representative of the whole? Above all—think first, write later.
Single Report	Similar to comprehensive (conceptually), but scope is very much more limited. Hard to keep balance. Findings not designed to describe what went right; therefore writer must use report summary to do this. See Figure 3 describing this single report process. Important caution—avoid feeble attempts at balancing.
Single Finding	Need not have the balance of whole report. Opening paragraph, however, should be self-standing like a summary of its own.
Briefing Memo	Can take any form but its brevity makes it very hard to keep a proper perspective.

Conclusion

Take particular care here. Don't let it be redundant and an unnecessary restatement of the problem or report. If nothing else, you may inject new unwanted emphases.

17

Recommendations: The "Onion Skin" Approach to Correct Specificity

The last group of diagrams in the auditor's "play book" is the set of recommendations. (I'll discuss the onion skin approach later.) These represent the culmination of all the preceding work–from the preliminaries where the scope and purpose were set, through the survey and verification stages, into the difficult summing up, and now, recommended actions. These could be either to the auditee, or to a client about the auditee.

For continued emphasis, let me return to my original hypotheses laid out in the Introduction. The end products (audit reports) should be practical blueprints of what needs fixing (operations and procedures), prospectively, and a reliable opinion of what needs adjusting (financial statements), retroactively.

PROFESSIONAL RECOMMENDATIONS AND THE SCOPE OF INQUIRY

Fixing any balance sheet or profit and loss statement line item is a relatively straightforward task requiring for the most part well-understood journal entries. If receivables were overstated because a supposedly large sale never was actually consummated—not much of a problem—debit (reduce) the sales account; credit (increase) accounts receivable; close it out by crediting sales; and debit an equity account. In effect, this merely reverses what was previously incorrectly entered. If prepaid insurance was inaccurately computed, adjust it. Most modern (and practical) small practitioners, by the way, hardly ever waste their time with entries for prepaid expenses or deferred income when auditing a continuously operating business. One could easily defend their rationale and also logically meet the test of consistent reporting. For example, after the first year of operation is concluded and the business continues a fairly steady pattern of operations, there will be a reasonably similar amount of new insurance being purchased as well as being "consumed." Why should the small practitioner waste time in preparing adjusting entries, back and forth, in this area. One could justify writing off as an expense, all new insurance premiums in the future, in total. It will generally even itself out after the first year of operation and only materially be significant in the last year of operation, or when the business is eventually sold or merged, which may be a long way off.

How to continue our discussion of recommendations? The most direct route to the main point is to retrace the logical steps that led from the start of each audit to the theoretical "end" (from setting the scope, to writing the report). However, the direct "key" to useful and professional recommendations is the scope. If the scope section is vague and the audit objectives are fuzzy, can a poor audit leading to inadequate recommendations be far behind?

One very important point must be made at the outset—the auditee has to be administratively equipped and sufficiently understanding, in a managerial sense, to carry out the business and procedural aspects of the necessary recommended changes revealed by the audit just finished. It is not enough for the auditor to *pontificate* and say certain things should be changed this way or that. He must say who should change them—how, and (realistically) whether they can be done with organizational resources at hand. Let me do two things to illustrate this general point.

SOME DO'S AND DON'TS

First, I would like to dish up some do's and dont's that might help the reader understand my thematic suggestions and avoid some unnecessary pitfalls.

Second, I would like to sketch out, afterwards, a pertinent case history, where the scope is clear and definitive. This is to show that–if all the audit steps followed the scope script and the verification of the surveyed indicators was precisely done and if the conditions and findings were properly described and summarized–then, the recommendations are a natural successor to this entire process. The auditor can then readily suggest to the client (or any involved reader) how these defects should be fixed. And he narrates the pertinent points. But to be fully useful, however, they must also be practical, timely (on-line), and directed to someone (or some group), or some layer of management that can actually and officially act on the suggestions in a practical way–be an "agent for change."

First, some examples of Do's and Don'ts.

> Do not tell an office manager to mechanize or computerize his (or her) accounting records when the treasurer of the firm has previously informed him of a severe corporate budget crunch resulting from recent unwise investments. Of course, it may be warranted and economically sound in the long run and under normal circumstances, but it certainly is not feasible now.
>
> Do not recommend better internal control mechanisms involving a textbook-sound separation of duties in a small firm where most of the employees have to "double in brass" in many duties. Of course, the bookkeeper should not also prepare the bank deposits and enter cash receipts coming into the

firm by mail or through courier. But what if there is no one else to do it? More reasonably, suggest an occasional internal check-out process by the manager and by all means express some concern if the bookkeeper is seriously underpaid (by current market comparison) and still stays on.

Do not just recommend vague overall improvements in the quality control check system in the manufacturing process or plant operations. Do report where the errors or malfunctions are occurring, and why, and how the present system is not adequately disclosing their origin.

Do not prescribe any adjusting journal entries without explanation of how the error occurred and what will prevent its recurrence. These, obviously, are only a handful of illustrations but should suffice to dramatize the point.

Now for an illustrative story. One might refer to this as the "onion skin" approach to recommendations. It involves the principle of leveling the suggested action deep enough (but not too far down) in the organization—or conversely not high enough—so that the manager or executive at the precisely right layer can, or is equipped to, take the corrective action that will do the job. Consider the following:

The auditor is assigned the task of checking out a large supermarket for reliability of controls (cash, inventory, personnel, etc.), and also the economy and efficiency of a large branch operation. He finds:

Ordering tactics are poor. The produce section manager keeps asking for only the most obvious day-to-day vegetables. This is not fully responsive to the store's clientele, which has a high-income and varied ethnic mix. The store's main competitor (easily observable) does a very high volume in specialty fruits and vegetables and meats. The meat and fish managers similarly stock only routine items, losing many potential customers.

There was relatively loose physical attention to the high-dollar, small-sized items such as spices, vitamins, and cigarettes in the back-up storage bins in the store's lockers.

Too many spoiled items were in evidence (for this type of store) in many of the food bins. Nobody, evidently, had specific instructions to periodically scan and remove these from the shelves (or see why they happened in the first place).

Public notices on the customer's bulletin board were either blatantly commercial (not store policy) or clearly outdated.

There was an abnormally high turnover rate among store employees. Also, when queried, no one presently on the job could recall any useful training sessions or short policy meetings to explain any regular store procedures.

The store manager was not properly implementing the company policy that permitted store employees to buy store merchandise at a 20 percent discount (a competitive fringe benefit advocated by the union and useful in attracting and keeping lower-level employees at little cost to management).

The store manager appeared unequipped to run this big outlet. He was, however, the best they could get because his official pay scale was not competitive with other stores nearby. This chain store set their manager's salaries based on sales.

The sales would always be depressed because only a really dynamic store manager could have instituted management and merchandizing techniques to raise the sales volume. But this would never happen because the low existing sales volume mandated the retention of, at best, a perfunctory manager. This is obviously a continuously self-defeating situation.

But this central store policy was set by the personnel section in the chain headquarters—and not analyzed or determined by any sales executive—a serious error. The personnel staff could not see beyond their own horizons. Any really effective audit recommendation in this instance had to go to some top executive—certainly not to the store manager, absolutely not to the personnel section. Moral of the story: Peel the onion, skin by skin, until the right layer becomes the real target.

POINT SHEET

RECOMMENDATIONS: THE "ONION SKIN" APPROACH TO CORRECT SPECIFICITY

Recommendation Content	Think them out carefully; just a few basic types: Adjust the accounts. Refund overcharges. Collect underpayments. Issue/refine policy.
Using the Onion Skin Approach	Peel the problem away layer by layer until you reach the proper layer for recommending corrective action. Be certain that your recommendations can be implemented. Face reality. Not all good things can come to pass. Don't pontificate. Do be specific.

PART SIX

The Education of an Auditor: The Need for a Broader Outlook

18

Why Auditors Should Be Only Part Accountant

Having recently earned your diploma, you approach your first job interview recalling that your were almost a straight-A student in your accounting subjects. People say you are very personable. This job should be a cinch to get! If asked, you would, after graduation, claim to be a qualified accountant. But are your really suited to being an auditor, which is what the prospective employers are looking for?

You know that you have a good touch for accounting. Why, even the so-called tough subjects—like corporate mergers or partnership dissolutions—came easy. But what's the difference between an auditor and an accountant; what's needed to be a successful auditor?

WHAT IS AN EDUCATED AUDITOR?

I've left this discussion for later because I would like it to help close the loop between thoughts at the end of the book and the opening remarks at the beginning. Therefore, let me go back to the beginning of the book where I outlined the attributes that I consider essential for a good auditor. They all relate in one way or another to the difference between an accountant and an auditor.

First, what can one say about native (or applied) intelligence? Candidly, either you have it or you don't. If you don't, it would be very useful to have a set of strong muscles, a seven-foot frame, exceptional hand-eye coordination, or a parent who has a successful business group. Possessing a real flair for pleasing others, or being able to interact positively with people in the arts, politics, selling, or related promotional fields might also be very useful or marketable characteristics.

But if one is heavily endowed with some real gray matter and is oriented toward business administration rather than science, medicine, or law, a satisfying and rewarding career in auditing is possible. Very few auditors are ever out of work. Other needed attributes (unlike native intelligence) can be acquired and enhanced if one studies and thinks about them in a positive way.

The second attribute that I would look for in an auditor candidate is interest in and curiosity about ideas and things. It never fails to amaze me how little curiosity some people have about the almost infinite number of fascinating things and processes there are in the world, how they work, what makes them fail, where they came from, how might they be changed, how one can make better use of them, and on and on!

As an interesting, but pertinent aside regarding curiosity, let me tell you a story about a highly successful friend of mine—likeable but with a short attention span—who happens to be a professional conference chairman. On a recent visit to California, some friends of hers escorted her and her husband to Muir Woods (outside of San Francisco) to see the world-famous grove of giant redwood trees there. There are hundreds of them; each one stately and picturesque. They present a truly spectacular show of nature on the grandest scale. But not for my friend. She got out of the car saying to her hosts, "This is great. Show me your biggest tree!" She looked at it, walked all around it, and was ready to leave. She didn't even try to hug this monster tree.

I think it's a great experience to be able to hug a 300-foot tree that is 75 feet around; even if you can only grab a small part of it. Now, this story may be apropos of nothing, or it may be a good example of the approach I am recommending to auditors, new and old. Be curious! Be interested!

A WORKABLE APPROACH FOR FINDING GOOD AUDITOR CANDIDATES

As concerns auditors in general and their need for the widest possible range of interest, I can well remember, some 15 years ago, discussing with the chief financial executive of a very large governmental department the need for raising the sights, capabilities, and perspectives of the audit staff. This was considered essential to enable them to cope with the almost infinite complexities and technical rigors involved in reviewing the operations of a very diverse business and social entity of major dimensions. (Just deciding *what* to review using standards of materiality and vulnerability was a heavy task in itself.) His main point was that auditors as a rule were the product of universities that endowed them with a pretty good grasp of accounting—but a very poor one of the related social and civic studies so essential to full understanding. Granted, there are many, many courses concerning such subjects as ADP, statistical sampling, and so on. However, these are not social or civic in content. What I am speaking about is taking an educated person in the liberal arts and then giving him or her a relatively easy technical skill (accounting). My interlocutor wanted to overcome this deficiency by recruiting, each semester, a special select group of very intelligent graduates (our first attribute) who had at least an A-minus average and who had degrees in any of the liberal arts (political science, language, history, philosophy, etc.). We would, as a form of high-level on-the-job training, send these graduates to a handpicked post-graduate business administration school to acquire sufficient credits in accounting (equivalent to an MBA) that would qualify them for a career in auditing. This composite training, which represented a great break with tradition, would presumably make for a well-rounded, good-thinking, and fully tempered auditor novice who could best cope with all the *social challenges*, which are the hardest part of this interesting profession. He was right on target!

I worked out this program for him with the help of a progressive "Renaissance dean" at a major university that had a good School of Public Administration. At this moment, many of these graduates are performing at very high levels in various important auditing and other managerial assignments, in private industry and government circles. Along these lines, it may be interesting to note that many large corporations insist that their brightest management interns (those tabbed for later important executive posts) must serve an early stint as corporate auditors. Many are not accountants (academically). That is, they have had, at most, only a modest number of credits in formal accounting courses.

THE MATERIALITY QUOTIENT

I have often wondered why certain people have a sure instinct for knowing what is important in any situation and an ability to separate the trivial from the significant. The whole subject of materiality is probably the murkiest, the most pervasive, and the most elusive of all the concepts embedded in the accounting standards and instructional texts.

I think one of the main thoughts underlying the whole novel educational effort just described was the executive's belief that students who spent their undergraduate years studying social sciences had more useful practice and were better equipped philosophically to deal with the very troublesome, but critical, overall subject of materiality. They had a better grasp of what is significant—and what is trivial.

What actually does the word *significant* mean? And how do you define *trivial*? Dictionaries will tell you that significant is not commonplace or trivial; and trivial is unimportant or commonplace. Not much help here.

On the other hand, students who wrestled frequently with these linguistic or philosophic nuances, if given the additional skills of accountancy, tend to make better reviewers or evaluators of business practices in the long run than do accountants who have had less or limited skills with or less intensive practice in solving tough, maybe vague, conceptual problems. I suppose that like pornography, "You know it when you see it." The truly balanced person will know (instinctively) when things are meaningful and deserve intensive attention—and when they are frivolous or unimportant. But balance is an instinctive trait—tightrope walking is an acquired skill—ask any circus performer.

DISTINGUISHING THE AUDITOR FROM THE ACCOUNTANT

There are two more ways I can think of that might explain the essence of what differentiates an accountant from an auditor. Consider first the "Transom Analogy." (I'm fond of detective and spy stories and can't resist using similar terminology.)

Picture the accounting office of the business entity or organization you are auditing for economy of operations as being housed in a closed room with no windows and an open transom on top of the locked door. The only ready contact with the outside world is through that open transom. People from the whole organization walk by any hour of night or day and toss pieces of paper into the open transom. The papers say we sold this, bought that, hired him, fired her, lost this, paid a bill (or ten thousand bills), transferred or manufactured these basic goods into finished pieces, sued so and so, contracted for such and such, and so much more. Maybe it isn't pieces of paper they toss in but computer tapes and reels that say the same thing.

The chief accountant in the room, who is very competent, in the most orderly way and in full compliance with all prescribed accounting principles, records every piece of information given him. This, traditionally, is what an *accountant* does. Obviously this is dramatically oversimplified, but the point is he records what he is furnished and cannot record what is not tossed in the transom.

Auditors are called on to do much, much more. They are expected to evaluate what is needed, how often, in what form, for whose use, and then they see to it that the mechanics of the bookkeeping are orderly and accurately carried out and that management reports of all types are responsive and material.

Here's another way of looking at the distinction between acountants and auditors. An accountant should be expert at keeping "book" on the data furnished by an organization. Now, think of this same accounting group as having an open transom, plus an open door, a telephone, and wide open windows! The accountant should now have two-way contact with his or her whole organization to see whether every business data need is being met.

This is part of what the auditor does—he or she evaluates what the accounting expert is doing and why. He also should be capable of seeing whether nonaccountants, such as the sales and engineering experts, know what they're doing and why.

The difference, then, is auditors should be expert at accounting (like accountants) and expert at judging whether any other expert seems on top of his job—not to substitute his expertise for theirs (as he can do in the accounting field) but to see if they can demonstrate the controlled logic in their field. This is why the auditor must be only part accountant. And this takes thinking, reading, inquisitiveness, understanding, exposure to all things and—oh yes—high intelligence to understand it all.

But, let me stress again one important, specific educational attribute that the modern auditor must have: hands-on expertise in computer programming. See Chapter 9, Computer Auditing, for the full discussion.

THE IMPACT OF CURRENT NARROW-SCOPE METHODS OF TEACHING ACCOUNTANTS

In concluding this chapter, let me thoughtfully inquire into the overall structure of accounting education. Stated otherwise, does the accounting graduate have, as standards prescribe, the technical ability to fulfill his or her responsibilities as a prospective auditor? The answer seems fairly clear that many new accountants find that their formal education did not adequately prepare them for these responsibilities. This is evidenced by the fact that a large portion of the training budget for newly hired accountants by public accounting firms and federal and state audit groups is spent in very basic curricula—sampling techniques, writing skills, interpretive analyses, computer auditing, and so on.

The research efforts of most accounting schools have largely neglected auditing practice; practitioners in and out of public or government practice find themselves unable to relate to most published accounting research and their related reports and articles—even textbooks. (If nothing else, they are dreadfully dull.) They turn to current national and state accounting journals. This is partly why this book was written—to help fill the void in understanding logical auditing and to provide a readable primer, without distracting references and tedious appendixes.

Almost every executive audit practitioner I know considers training, as I do, to be very important to the would-be successful practitioner. As a practical aid, I would like to include at this point a "Composite Training Profile" which I previously initiated. It can serve as a handy training reference for auditors at various rungs on their career ladder. It covers fundamental audit duties at all working levels from entry to managing auditors. The profile recognizes the ever-increasing difficulties in modern business—especially the heavy need for auditor training in EDP aspects, professional standards, and such subjects as sampling, working papers, and supervision.

TRAINING OVERVIEW

To restate a fundamental characteristic of an audit staff: Entry level auditors generally bring to their organizations a basic college or university educational background or its equivalent that all too often has not sufficiently prepared the auditor/investigator to effectively perform the audit function. Therefore, we must build upon the college education by providing a well-rounded auditor training program.

How do we do this? There are four critical elements. One must:

Determine what is expected (fundamental audit duties) of auditors at all levels–junior through executive senior (Chart 1).

Establish a (perhaps automated) Personal/Individual Employee Profile comparing the training needs of the staff to training already provided (Chart 2).

Identify the existing Training Delivery Systems available to provide auditor training needs on an individualized basis (Chart 3).

Develop curricula of training courses emphasizing relevant professional auditing standards and accounting principles affecting fundamental audit duties (Chart IV).

Charts 1 through 4 are examples of these, developed for a large federal audit group. They are adaptable to any audit staff.

CHART 1
BASIC AUDIT DUTIES

Junior

Follow orders
Prepare workpapers
Conduct interviews and write-up interviews
Schedule Data
Follow audit guides

Semisenior

Prepare audit guides/programs
Supervise entry-level staff
Function as auditor-in-charge
Prepare written reports containing findings and recommendations

Develop findings
Conduct entrance and exit conferences
Identify and report fraud
Use statistical sampling

Senior

Run jobs (often more than one)
Write reports
Manage branch office or equivalent
Rate and review staff
Plan, formulate, and develop policies and audit standards
Insure quality assurance standards
Deal with fraud (conceptually)

Supervising Senior

Manage branches and divisions
Represent the Audit Office in the profession
Apply professional standards and teach them
Communicate to the executive level of management
Testify, if necessary, at hearings or in courtroom proceedings
Develop new policies and procedures for audit

Manager/Executive

Render technical advice at the managing level
Establish and direct audit policy
Represent the profession
Serve on professional committees and subcommittees
Teach at a high level
Lecture to academic, public, and business groups
Be able to rule on technical matters
Write articles for professional journals
Participate at top-level business decisions and operations.

CHART 2
EMPLOYEE AUDITOR TRAINING PROFILE

Section 1 Identification

1. Name and other pertinent personal data

Section 2. Education

2. Degree
3. Year
4. Institution
5. Major
6. Minor

Section 3. Training

7. Course/Program and date

   A. ______________________________
   B. ______________________________
   C. ______________________________
   D. ______________________________
   E. ______________________________

8. Level when taken

   A. ______________________________
   B. ______________________________
   C. ______________________________
   D. ______________________________
   E. ______________________________

9. Institution/Location

   A. ______________________________
   B. ______________________________
   C. ______________________________
   D. ______________________________
   E. ______________________________

Section 4. Professional Certification

10. CPA
11. CIA
12. Bar
13. Other professional certification

Section 5. Professional Activities

14. Organization titles

Section 6. Job Assignment History

15. Office/division

    A. ______
    B. ______
    C. ______
    D. ______

16. Geographic location

    A. ______
    B. ______
    C. ______
    D. ______

17. Number of years

    A. ______
    B. ______
    C. ______
    D. ______

Section 7. Assignment Preferences/Reservations

18. Preferences

    ______
    ______
    ______

19. Reservations

    ______
    ______
    ______

Section 8. Organization Location Preference

20. Organizational component

    A. ______
    B. ______
    C. ______

CHART 3
AUDITOR TRAINING DELIVERY SYSTEMS

Training Supplier

Office of Personnel Management
United States Department of Agriculture
Interagency Auditor Training Program
Defense Contract Audit Agency
Association of Government Accountants
Department of Defense Computer Institute
American Institute of Certified Public Accountants
American Management Association
The George Washington University
National Association of Accountants
Institute of Internal Auditors
American University
Federal Law Enforcement Training Center
Department of the Army Civilian Career Development Program
Association of Federal Investigators

Note: The following compendium was designed to illustrate the training sources representative of the kinds of auditor training opportunities generally available in public quarters. This list can be greatly ampified by adding private training courses. It is intended to reinforce principally the point regarding the huge need for auditor training after graduation from college.

CHART 4
LISTING OF TRAINING COURSES AVAILABLE TO AUDITORS IN A LARGE FEDERAL AGENCY (VARIOUS SUPPLIERS)

1. General Subjects

Conducting Program Results Reviews, Based on Techniques Developed by the U.S. General Accounting Office
Developing and Presenting Audit Findings
Effective Governmental Auditing
Operational Auditing
Operational Auditing, Based on Techniques Developed by the U.S. General Accounting Office

Principles of Audit operations
The Freedom of Information Act and the Privacy Act
Conduct of Management Surveys
Implementation of the Freedom of Information and Privacy Acts
Cost Principles Applicable to Grants and Contracts with State and Local Governments
The Prevention and Detection of Fraud and Abuse—An Awareness Course for Auditors
Uniform Administrative Requirements for Grant-in-Aid to State and Local Governments
Basic Orientation
Basic Contract Audit Orientation
Technical Indoctrination
Working Papers Preparation
Intermediate Contract Auditing
Cost Accounting Standards
Introduction to Cost Accounting Standards
DOD Cost Accounting Standards Workshop
Advanced Cost Accounting Standards
Budgets Seminar
Operations Audits—Self-Study
Audits of Terminated Contracts
Surveillance of Cost Schedule Control Systems
Contract Performance Measurement
Defense Contract Negotiation Workshop
Defense Advanced Incentive Contracting Workshop
Advanced Auditing Techniques
Audit Evidence—Deciding How Much and What Type
Independent Auditor, Quality Control and General Standards
Field Work and Internal Control
Evidential Matter
Dating of Independent Auditor's Report Utilization Work of Other Auditors
Inadequate Disclosure, Inconsistency and Other Information
Detection of Errors or Illegal Acts
Compilation and Review of Financial Statements
Compilation and Review of Financial Statements, Lecture Program
Work Papers Review
Series on Auditing Federally Assisted Programs
Audit Diagnostic Review
General Standards (Auditing)
Standards of Field Work
Self-Study—Statements on Auditing Standards
Self-Study—Overview of an Audit and Write-up Engagement

Internal Auditing I—Tools and Techniques
Internal Auditing II—Audit Practices and Opportunities
Operational Auditing Seminar and Workshop
Developing and Organizing Audit Evidence—Attributes I
Presenting Audit Findings—Attributes II
Preparing Audit Reports—Attributes III
Use of Standardized Audit Guides—Finance/Compliance, Economy, Efficiency, Program Results
Systems Analysis for Government Results
Effective Treatment of Audit Findings
Audit and Accounting Standards
Operational Auditing—Basic
What Operational Auditing Is
Operational Auditing—Advanced
Basic Seminar Series on Government Auditing
Audit and Accounting Standards
The Detection and Prevention of Fraud and Abuse in Government
White Collar Crime Seminar
Strengthening Interviewing Skills
Operational Auditing
Basic Financial Statement Analysis
Leadership Skills for Project Managers
Operational Auditing

2. Statistics for Auditors

Practical Statistical Sampling for Auditors
Correlation and Regression Analysis
Practical Statistics
Statistical Sampling in Government Operations
Statistical Techniques for Analysis
Introductory Statistics I
Introductory Statistics II
Introductory Statistics III
Introduction to Survey Methods
Theory of Sample Surveys I
Theory of Sample Surveys II
Introduction to Statistics
Descriptive Statistics I
Descriptive Statistics II
Statistical Sampling Techniques Workshop
Self-Study—Elements of Statistics
Sample Survey Methods

Self-Study–Statistical Sampling
Statistical Sampling
Basic Graphic Analysis
Basic Improvement Curve
Graphic, Computational and Improvement Curve Analysis Techniques
Self-Study–An Auditors Approach to Statistical Sampling Series
Statistical Sampling Seminar and Workshop
Simplified Probability Sampling
Statistical Sampling for Accountants and Auditors
Introduction to Statistical in Auditing
Planning, Designing, Supervising and Applying Statistical Audit Samples
Audit Applications of Dollar-Unit and Random Moment Sampling and Correlation-Regression Analysis

3. Audit-Supervisory

Planning, Managing and Reporting for Audit Managers and Supervisors
Seminar for Audit Managers
Statistical Sampling for Audit Managers and Supervisors
Defense Procurement Executive Seminar
Applied Supervision
Managerial Roles in Human Organizations
Seminar for New Managers
Seminar for Advancing Managers
The Director's Fellowship Program in Management
Senior Defense Resources Management
Conferences for Senior Executives on Public Policy Issues
Conference on Business in Contemporary Society
Senior Executive Education Program
Managing the Reporting Process
The Executive Leadership and Management Program
Orientation in Systems and Acquisition
Pre-Leadership Training–Self-Study
Supervision and Technical Management
Supervision and Group Performance
Management and Group Performance
Basic Management Methods and Skills
Audit Manager's Seminar
Audit Supervisor's Development Course
Audit Manager's Seminar–Special Topics
Behavioral Aspects of Government Accounting and Accountants
Principles of Management for Government Auditors and Accountants
Principles of Managerial Economics for Government Auditors

Productivity Work Measurement Standards, Measurement and Evaluation
Setting and Implementing Management Goals and Objectives
Developing Supervisory Leadership Skills
Advanced Management Skills and Techniques for First Line Supervision

4. ADP

An Introduction to ADP
Executive Seminar to ADP
Management Introduction to ADP
Design of a Computerized Management Information System
Security and Privacy of Computer Systems
Federal Financial Management Information Systems
Auditing Automated Systems: Tools & Techniques
Auditing On-Line Systems
Auditing Systems Supported by ADP Equipment I
Auditing Systems Supported by ADP Equipment II
Automated Financial Systems Series
Automated Personal Systems
Management Information Systems
Getting the System Management: A User's Guide to Project Management
Computer Crime, Fraud, and Embezzlement: An Update on Current EDP Trends
Computer Security, A Management Blindspot? An Update on Current EDP Trends
Computer Security—Protecting People, Hardware, Records: An Update on Current EDP Trends
Data Processing Concepts
Computer Performance Evaluation
Information Systems Analysis and Design
ADP I
Advanced ADP Program
ADP II
EDP and Internal Control
Computer Control and Auditing
EDP Introduction I
EDP II
EDP Introduction to COBOL
Basic Programming Language
Operating Systems and Job Control Language
Database Workshop
Data Communications Workshop
Systems Design Workshop

Computer Control and Auditing–An Introduction
Introduction to EDP Concepts and Controls
Basic Computer Concepts and Controls–Self-Study
System Development Life-Cycle Seminar
EDP Audit and Control I–Computer Background
EDP Audit and Control II–Controls, Systems, Security and Audit Opportunities
EDP Unit and Control III–Audit Techniques
Auditing Computerized Systems
Computer Fraud and Abuse–Preventative
Auditing of EDP Centers
Using Computers as an Audit Tool
Auditing with Computer Performance Evaluation
Computer System Security
System Performance Evaluation
Operational Audit of the EDP Function
Computer Performance Evaluation, People Hardware User Satisfaction
EDP Auditing Concepts and Techniques
Fundamentals of Data Processing for Accounting and Financial Managers
Computer Security and Internal Control
Fundamentals of Data Processing for Accounting and Financial Managers
Computer Security and Internal Control
Managing Computer System Security
The Privacy Act and Information Systems

5. Special Techniques and Skills

Report Writing Workshop
Writing Analytical Reports
Flow Charting for Auditors
Interviewing Techniques for Auditors
Successful Audit Report Writing
Written Communication for Auditors
English Composition
Introduction to Research Report Writing
Fundamentals of Written Communication
Writing to Communicate
Effective Writing–A Seminar
Government Report and Letter Writing–A Seminar
Editing. A Workshop for Managers and Supervisors
Flow Charting
Self-Study–How to Run Productive Meetings
Audit Report Writing

Effective Reading Course
Rapid Reading
Interpersonal Communication Skills Workshop
Self-Study—Standards of Reporting and the Auditor's Standard Report
Self-Study—Communication Skills for Managers
Effective Writing for Accountants and Auditors
Presentation Techniques
How to Sharpen Your Business Writing Skills
Communications and Report Writing
Your Communication Skills and Techniques

POINT SHEET

THE EDUCATION OF AN AUDITOR (THE NEED FOR A BROADER OUTLOOK)

An Auditor Is Not Just an Accountant

An accountant has a strong background and grasp of accounting theory and practice and related commercial subjects.

The auditor must have these same qualifications but needs more, much more.

Communication and observation skills, knowledge of computers and scientific sampling, knowledge about professional standards, various industry differences and structures, tax laws and basic legal arrangements, staff management and related personnel administration, flow charting and staff planning techniques (the list is long).

Some of these attributes can be (but are not generally) acquired during the college years through classroom training. This slack must be overcome by the employer of the young auditor through formal classroom courses.

Other attributes can be acquired through patient seasoning by on-the-job training.

Others can be self-taught. Learn to be curious!

Read and think. Almost everything you see and hear will be useful on some audit somewhere.

The Materiality Quotient: If There Is Any One Word in the Audit World More Important Than Any Other, It's Materiality

How do you separate the forest from the trees in assessing the significance of various matters? Taking note of the world around you seems to be the answer.

Thoughts on Improving Audit Staff Capabilities

Determine what is expected of you and your audit staff at all levels.

Develop an individual training profile on each staff member.

Seek out training systems available.

Identify courses being offered.

At the executive level give training high priority. (It is not discardable overhead.)

19

The "Stillman's Gym" Approach to Training

I would like the reader to accept this chapter as a short and exhortative analogy intended to encourage practicing professionals and teachers to train, train, train, which means think, think, think.

Why the reference to New York City's Stillman's Gym? Back in the 1930s, Stillman's was a mecca for both the would-be aspiring boxers and the already scarred, professional boxers who daily went there to sharpen their pugilistic skills. They skipped rope; grunted out sit-ups, push-ups, and warm-ups; shadow boxed and sparred mates; pummelled bags; sparred with anyone they could find—daily and with fanatic persistence. Times were bad, but they kept in shape waiting for any call for arms.

I ask professional auditors, everywhere, to also go to Stillman's everyday. Train! Write! Study other good writers! Master the mechanics of everyday sampling and analyze various higher-level mathematical applications. Familiarize yourself with computers and make their mysteries a thing of the past. But above all, think—about people, their habits, about new (or old) administrative and economic systems, about everything. Keep yourself sharp. It will all be useful at some time, in some place, during some audit. If nothing else, your client and their managers will be able to rely on you to simulate, in your mind, *their* problems and *their* rationale for doing things the way they do, or maybe why they do not do them the way you or others might prefer.

20

Standards: The Mark of a Profession

During the entire course of this text, I have tried to help the reader to more fully and deeply understand the nature of auditing by pointing out how logical and how closely related to everyday happenings its processes are. The adoption of logical techniques and applications must in itself result in a more useful and professional audit report. Similarly, when we come to the subject of standards, my studies have convinced me that this is where the highest expression of the logic of the auditing business comes to the fore. Why?

First, the principal auditing authorities (the American Institute of CPAs, the General Accounting Office, and the Institute of Internal Auditors) have each promulgated a set of formal auditing standards that they expect their members to abide by in accomplishing every audit. (Other groups are following suit). This requirement is obviously logical and necessary. The crucial distinguishing factor that separates craftsmen, technicians, performers, and artisians from responsive professionals is rigorous standards, such as those followed by lawyers, doctors, engineers, and auditors!

Second, the standards set forth by these main groups are responsive to the special needs to each; they are logical and are very well thought out.

Third, although the AICPA Codification of Statements on Auditing Standards is voluminous and somewhat intimidating to practitioners and students, its many parts can be sorted out and related to the main phases of auditing and all their underlying concepts. I would like to provide a full analysis and detailed Point Sheet for the reader in this closing chapter as a summation of the entire proceeding narration.

In general and to begin with, since standards are a formal expression, who, precisely, issues them?

Statements on Auditing standards are issued by the AICPA's Auditing Standards Board, the senior technical body of the Institute designated to issue pronouncements on auditing matters. Rule 202 of the Institute's Code of Professional Ethics requires adherence to the applicable generally accepted auditing standards promulgated by the Institute. It recognizes Statements on Auditing Standards as interpretations of generally accepted auditing standards and requires that members be prepared to justify departures from such Statements. When the Auditing Standards Board was formed as the successor to prior senior technical committees on auditing matters, it was given the following charge:

> The AICPA Auditing standards Board shall be responsible for the promulgation of auditing standards and procedures to be observed by members of the AICPA in accordance with Institute's rules of conduct.
>
> The Board shall be alert to new opportunities for auditors to serve the public, both by the assumption of new responsibilities and by improved ways of meeting old ones, and shall as expeditiously as possible develop standards and procedures that will enable the auditor to assume those responsibilities.
>
> Auditing standards and procedures promulgated by the Board shall:
>
> > Define the nature and extent of the auditor's responsibilities.

Provide guidance to the auditor in carrying out his duties, enabling him to express an opinion on the reliability of the representations on which he is reporting.

Make special provision, where appropriate, to meet the needs of small enterprises.

Have regard to the costs which they impose on society in relation to the benefits reasonably expected to be derived from the audit function.

The Auditing Standards Board shall provide auditors with all possible guidance in the implementation of its pronouncements, by means of interpretations of its statements, by the issuance of guidelines, and by any other means available to it.

As for the GAO, the comptroller general of the United States, under his individual authority, issued standards in February 1981, revising the 1972 and 1974 editions and generally embodying the AICPA Standards. They are under further revision at the time of this writing. There are some important distinctions which I will discuss later. Since it is short and important, the foreword to the GAO Standards is hereby presented in its entirety.

During the 1960s both the number and dollar amounts of government programs increased substantially. These programs were aimed at improving the quality of American life. In the 1970s the number of new programs established was considerably less, but the total dollar amount continued to grow. This increase in government programs brought with it an increased demand for full accountability by those entrusted with the responsibility for administering the programs. Auditing is an integral element of this accountability, and governments are responsible for ensuring that appropriate audits are made.

In the past few years, we have seen an unprecedented interest in government auditing. Public officials, legislators, and private citizens want and need to know not only whether government funds are handled properly and in compliance with laws and regulations, but also whether government organizations are achieving the purposes for which programs were authorized and funded and are doing so economically and efficiently.

Forty years ago auditors concentrated most of their efforts on auditing the vouchers which supported expenditures. But today, auditors are also concerned with the economy, efficiency, and effectiveness of government operations.

Auditing plays an important role in government since it is a management tool for evaluating whether operations are executed economically, efficiently, and effectively. While it is true that auditors have the responsibility to evaluate government operations, management cannot and should not completely rely on the auditors to detect problems and recommend solutions. The auditors cannot do it all. Therefore government managers, as part of their management responsibiity, must routinely assess their own operations to assure themselves, their superiors, legislators, and private citizens that operations are well controlled and meet high expectations. If problems are found, by the auditor or by management, it is management's responsibility to act promptly and properly to initiate corrective action.

In 1972 the U.S. General Accounting Office (GAO) issued "Standards for Audit of Governmental Organizations, Programs, Activities & Functions," better known as the "yellow book." Since issuing the standards, GAO has issued publications explaining and supplementing the standards and demonstrating how auditing can improve the efficiency and effectiveness of government operations and programs. These publications are identified on the inside of the front cover.

The standards as issued in 1972 have proved to be sound and durable and have been generally accepted by all levels of government as well as by the accounting profession. The Office of Management and Budget (OMB) has cited the standards in OMB circulars as basic audit criteria for Federal executive departments and agencies to follow. Also, Federal legislation requires that the inspectors general follow the standards.

These standards have been revised in order to:

1. *Expand the explanations of some standards in response to questions about them.*
2. *Separate the standards for financial and compliance audits from those for economy and efficiency audits and program results audits.*
3. *Incorporate standards relating to audits in which automatic data processing systems are used by the entity.*
4. *Add a standard to make more specific the auditor's responsibility for detecting fraud and abuse in government programs and operations.*

This revision of the standards is based on comments and suggestions that GAO has received since the standards were originally issued. These comments and suggestions were considered in preparing a draft of the revised standards which was sent to audit officials at all levels of government, the public accounting profession, professional organizations, academia, and other interested groups and persons for review and comment. The comments received were reviewed and incorporated as appropriate in these final revised standards.

We are grateful to those government officials, professional organizations, public accounting officials, and members of the academic community who have commented on the standards.

This edition of the standards supersedes the 1972 and 1974 editions of the standards and the March 1979 booklet entitled "Additional GAO Audit Standards, Auditing Computer-Based Systems."

Elmer B. Staats
Comptroller General
of the United States

February 27, 1981

The International Professional Standards and Responsibilities Committee of the Institute of Internal Auditors issued their standards in 1977, which are also being revised. For the same reasons as above, I have included their formal Introduction for emphasis and for the reader's convenience.

Internal auditing is an independent appraisal function established within an organization to examine and evaluate its activities as a service to the organization. The objective of internal auditing is to assist members of the organization in the effective discharge of their responsibilities. To this end, internal auditing furnishes them with analyses, appraisals, recommendations, counsel, and information concerning the activities reviewed.

The members of the organization assisted by internal auditing include those in management and the board of directors. Internal auditors owe a responsibility to both, providing them with information about the adequacy and effectiveness of the organization's system of internal control and the quality of performance. The information furnished to each may differ in format and detail, depending upon the requirements and requests of management and the board.

The internal auditing department is an integral part of the organization and functions under the policies established by management and the board. The statement of purpose, authority, and responsibility (charter) for the internal auditing department, approved by management and accepted by the board, should be consistent with these Standards for the Professional Practice of Internal Auditing.

The charter should make clear the purposes of the internal auditing department, specify the unrestricted scope of its work, and declare that auditors are to have no authority or responsibility for the activities they audit.

Throughout the world internal auditing is performed in diverse environments and within organizations which vary in purpose, size, and structure. In addition, the laws and customs within various countries differ from one another. These differences may affect the practice of internal auditing in each environment. The implementation of these Standards, therefore, willl be governed by the environment in which the internal auditing department carries out its assigned responsibilities. But compliance with the concepts enunciated by these *Standards* is essential before the responsibilities of internal auditors can be met.

"Independence," as used in these Standards, requires clarification. Internal auditors must be independent of the activities they audit. Such independence permits internal auditors to perform their work freely and objectively. Without independence, the desired results of internal auditing cannot be realized.

In setting these Standards, the following developments were considered:

1. *Boards of directors are being held increasingly accountable for the adequacy and effectiveness of their organizations' systems of internal control and quality of performance.*
2. *Members of management are demonstrating increased acceptance of internal auditing as a means of supplying objective analyses, appraisals, recommendations, counsel, and information on the organization's controls and performance.*
3. *External auditors are using the results of internal audits to complement their own work where the internal auditors have provided suitable evidence of independence and adequate, professional audit work.*

In the light of such developments, the purposes of these Standards are to:

1. *Impart an understanding of the role and responsibilities of internal auditing to all levels of management, boards of directors, public bodies, external auditors, and related professional organizations*
2. *Establish the basis for the guidance and measurement of internal auditing performance*
3. *Improve the practice of internal auditing*

The Standards differentiate among the varied responsibilities of the organization, the internal auditing department, the director of internal auditing, and internal auditors.

The five general Standards are expressed in italicized statements in upper case. Following each of these general *Standards* are specific standards expressed in italicized statements in lower case. Accompanying each specific standard are guidelines describing suitable means of meeting that standard. The *Standards* encompass:

1. *The independence of the internal auditing department from the activities audited and the objectivity of internal auditors*
2. *The proficiency of internal auditors and the professional care they should exercise*
3. *The scope of internal auditing work*
4. *The performance of internal auditing assignments*
5. *The management of the internal auditing department*

The Standards and the accompanying guidelines employ three terms which have been given *specific* meanings. These are as follows:

The term board includes boards of directors, audit committees of such boards, heads of agencies or legislative bodies to whom internal auditors report, boards of governors or trustees of nonprofit organizations, and any other designated governing bodies of organizations.

The terms director of internal auditing and *director* identify the top position in an internal auditing department.

The term internal auditing department includes any unit or activity within an organization which performs internal auditing functions.

Let me conclude this section on Standards by saying that my regular Point Sheet, following this chapter, should serve to graphically guide the reader through the principle elements and organization of the various (and voluminous) codifications of the Standards. Without this type of road map, they tend to intimidate the student and overwhelm the general practitioner. Recent articles, various workshops, seminars, and lectures, and the call for widespread training show the increasing concern over possible "overloading" inherent in the whole situation and the need for simplication.

If it helps, one could make an interesting analogy between the methods employed by students of the Bible seeking guidance and auditors attempting to understand and comply with their professional standards. Regarding the Bible, most theologians will agree that the Ten Commandments represent the basic message and the full text (or texts) itself serves to explain, enlarge upon, inspire, and narrate historical happenings. Many learned religious leaders comment on the fundamental statements. Students who limit themselves to repetitive readings of the historical details and prescriptions and who commit much of them to memory, without relating them to the overriding concepts and inspirations, may lose sight of the principles.

So with the Standards. Merely concentrating heavily on all the details, seeking an answer for any or all possible audit situations, or for each condition encountered in the course of varied engagements should be, obviously, self-defeating—or at least unnecessarily complicated.

Therefore, let me ask the readers to similarly consider all eight points in my Point Sheet as being very important for a grasping of all the Audit Standards. As detailed in the accompanying Point Sheet, these form the keynotes for the Standards and can, in many different ways, be associated with most of the detailed items specified in the various codes.

Appropriate to the entire preceding text, all this ends on the keynote: "Above all else, (the auditor) stands or falls on his own *independent* opinion."

POINT SHEET

STANDARDS

The Following Lists and Compares the Responsibilities and Functions of Independent Auditors as promulgated by the American Institute of Certified Public Accountants (AICPA), the General Accounting Office (GAO), and the Institute of Internal Auditors, Inc. (IIA): First, the Auditor's Role

Per AICPA	Primary purpose: To render an independent opinion through a report on the financial position (of management), results of operations, and changes in financial position. All work must be done in accordance with the Standards. All work done in conformity with generally accepted accounting principles.
Per GAO	Embraces the essence of all Standards prescribed by the AICPA for financial audits, but includes additional standards for audits with an "expanded" scope dealing with compliance with laws and regulations, economy and efficiency, and program results.
Per IIA	Primary purpose: To provide an independent appraisal function *within* an organization to examine and evaluate the activities of the orgranization. Though specifically promulgated by IIA, these standards are much the same as those put forth by AICPA, and GAO, in that they call for objectivity, professional care, proficiency, and reliability.
Eight Important Thoughts and Concepts That Should Be Highlighted	With respect to evidentiary matters: The AICPA Standards call for such evidence to be "persuasive." Such evidence relates to audits of financial statements. GAO, which calls for audits involving compliance, economy, efficiency, and program results, requires more evidence—"reasonable assurance." The differences between these two definitions are most important. Cost barrier—AICPA states that if the auditor cannot satisfactorily complete an audit in full accordance with

the Standards because of fee restriction, he must disengage, limit the scope, or limit his opinion. (This statement is not emphasized in GAO or IIA.)

Vulnerability assessments must relate to items involving the disbursement of cash and ADP data ultimately affecting cash.

Auditors must do whatever is necessary to detect gross errors or gross misapplications. This requires due professional care based on adequate training.

Critical differences recognized between accounting controls (processes) and administration controls (which concern major functions). Administrative controls are more important.

Auditors are admonished: Don't deceive the reader of your report in any way.

All work must be timely; nothing works well if the audit effort is not "on-line."

The auditor's own judgment must prevail above all else. He (or she) stands or falls, ultimately, on his own independent opinions.

AICPA Standards–In Particular: Overall One Must Keep in Mind the Fundmental Differences between "Managment's" Responsibilities and those of the Independent Auditor

Management is Required to	Have sound accounting policies.
	Have a cohesive system of accounts.
	Safeguard assets (physically and through controlling records).
	Have proper financial statements reflecting the above.

On Each Assignment the Auditor's Main Responsibility Is to Offer a Clear Opinion of the Financial Statements. To Do This He Must

Be sufficiently educated (formal) and trained (on the job). Keep abreast of new professional pronouncements.

Exercise judgment in determining which auditing procedures are necessary in each circumstance to enable a clear opinion to be offered.

As a General Rule, Auditors Have an Overriding Responsibility to the *Profession* That is Represented by the AICPA through its Published Standards.

There Are a Number of "Generally Accepted" Standards, Conceptual in Nature, Referred to in Various Sections of the Codification. Some Main Points

Standards differ from *procedures* in that

Standards concern "quality of performance."

Standards require judgment be exercised on which procedures (or acts) are to be performed.

Auditors must (again) have adequate education (formal) and technical training (on the job). This includes formal education and supervised field work. Auditors are personally responsible for studying and understanding new professional pronouncements.

Auditors must be intellectually honest (mental attitude) and—be recognized as independent. They must also exercise due professional care—both in examination and the preparation of their report.

All the Standards relate to materiality and relative risk. Additionally, auditors must pay attention to important items.

Reports should state

Whether financial statements were (1) prepared in accordance with generally accepted accounting principles, and (2) whether these principles were consistently observed in the current period and in relation to the preceding period.

Whether financial statements are fully informative. If not, this condition must be fully discussed.

An opinion of the whole financial condition or a statement that such an opinion cannot be expressed (with the appropriate reason).

A clear-cut indication of the nature of an individual auditor's examination and the degree of responsibility, if that auditor's name is noted in the report.

There Are Seven Specific Standards Concerning "Due Professional Care"–(3 Field Work; 4 Reporting) These Form the Bulk of the AICPA Codification of Statements on Auditing Standards

Field Work

1st Standard–due professional care.

2d Standards–internal controls.

3d Standard–evidence.

Reporting

1st Standard–adherence.

2d Standard–consistency.

3d Standard–adequacy.

4th Standard–composite of a number of elements.

Field Work: 1st Standard (Due Professional Care)

Planning should provide for on-line (timely) audit work (simultaneous cash and security counts, current taking of inventories, for example).

	It should provide adequate supervision, including a knowledge of the entities' business.
2d Standard (Internal Controls)	Notes the difference between the need for opinions on financial statements and constructive suggestions to clients. Also the standard makes a very important distinction between accounting controls and actual processes. The standard further discusses the requirements for Safeguarding of assets. Reliability of financial records. A system of audit and approval. Separation of duties. Recordkeeping. Custody controls over operational assets. Management's Administrative Controls. The Standards discuss what should be expected as to: Supervision by management. The methods used in data gathering. Personnel qualifications and attributes such as competence, integrity, and independence. Separation of "functions." This is even more important than clean accounting controls since top management can overrule or subvert operations. Auditors need worry more about these than accounting controls.
3d Standard (Evidence)	In general, there are four main areas: inspections, inquiries, observations, and confirmations. Most of an independent auditor's effort in forming opinions consists of evaluating evidence and assertions in financial

statements. The validity of such evidence rests on the auditor's judgment and differs from legal evidence. Audit evidence is only pertinent if it is:

Objective.

Timely (on-line).

Corroborated.

Added notes on quality/content evidence:

Do assets or liabilities really exist at a given date (finished goods, inventories on the balance sheet available for sale)?

Did recorded transactions actually occur during a given period? For example, do sales totals in the income statement represent an exchange of goods or services with customers for cash or other consideration?

The validity of evidence must be gauged by the auditor's judgment. The auditor should consider the specific circumstances of the entity.

Audit procedures may derive from more than one audit objective.

Internal accounting controls and materiality must be considered.

Timing is important (e.g., don't check manufacturing costs during a plant shutdown).

Nature of the evidence.

Accounting data alone are not sufficient, but are still important.

Checks, invoices, contracts, inspections, physical examinations—all add to reliability.

Accounting records must show internal consistency.

They may include interviews of all kinds of people, in and out of the company.

Competence of the evidence.

Outside verification often provides greater assurance.

The auditor's direct knowledge of operations is very persuasive.

Because of the insufficiency of the evidence, it may be necessary to rely on evidence that is persuasive rather than conclusive (one principle difference between GAO and AICPA).

An experienced auditor is seldom convinced beyond all doubt.

Auditor works within economic limits. (f there is not enough time, continue to render an opinion, but confine it to what's been done.

A rational relationship should exist between the cost of obtaining evidence and the usefulness of the information obtained, but difficulty and expense are not in themselves a valid basis for omitting a test (again, consider relative risk).

Integrity of management: Does it have a history or reputation for overriding control procedures?

Adequate planning, timely field work, and early appointments are advantageous.

Timely (on-line) work during the year makes balance sheet work at the end of the year easier.

Items like cash, securities, and bank loans require simultaneous examination or surprise counts; timely inventory counts are a must.

Reporting (Four Standards)

Adherence

Reports should be developed in adherence to generally accepted accounting principles.

Consistency

Reports shall state whether such principles were consistently observed in the current period in relation to the preceding period.

Adequacy

Information disclosures in financial statements are to be regarded as reasonably adequate unless otherwise stated.

A composite of diverse elements are discussed:

When the accountant's name is to be associated with the financial statements.

The need for comparative financial statements.

Audited financial statements.

The policy as to dating the audit report.

A discussion of other conditions that preclude certain procedures.

A discussion of other auditor's examination.

Lack of conformity.

Inadequate disclosure.

Inconsistency.

Other information.

When to use condensed statements.

For emphasis, the report should express an opinion about financial statements taken as a whole, or explain why not. Where the auditor's name is associated with the report, there should be a clear-cut indication of the extent of the auditor's examination and the degree of his responsibility.

1st Standard (Adherence to Generally Accepted Accounting Principles)

The Standard includes not only accounting principles and practices but methods of applying them.

Cautionary note: The determination that a particular accounting principle is generally accepted may be difficult because no single reference source exists for all such principles. The various sources of established accounting principles are generally the following:

Pronouncements of an authoritative body designated by an AICPA Council to establish these principles, that is, FASB statements, FASB interpretations, accounting principles, Board opinions, AICPA accounting research bulletins, interpretations, audit guides, statements of position, concepts, and so on.

Bodies of expert accountants that distribute explanatory material.

Accounting literature, books, articles, monographs, and the like.

In all the above matters, substance rules over form.

2d Standard (Consistency)

Comparison between years may be affected by:

Accounting changes.

Error in a previous statement.

Changes in classification.

Substantially different events or transactions.

Examples are given of accounting changes:

Straight-line method to the declining balance, and so forth; an ad-

	vance in the reporting entity; combined statements versus individual comparisons.
	Newly arranged pooling of interest.
	As an example of classification, change working capital to cash or cash equivalent.
3d Standard (Adequacy)	If any required information is omitted, a qualified or adverse opinion is required.
	The basic rule of thumb is that the reader gets all information and that all disclosures should be reasonably adequate.
	The auditor must use careful judgment in making a disclosure on segmented information and stating whether it is material to whole or not.
4th Standard (Composite of a Number of Elements)	Objective is to prevent misinterpretation of the degree of responsibility accountant assumes when his name is associated with financial statements.
GAO Standards Incorporate AICPA Standards and Procedures and GAO Prescribes Additional Standards for Audits of Expanded Scope	
Three Elements of Expanded Scope Auditing Are	Financial statements present the financial position fairly. Determination must be made as to whether the entity
	Complies with laws and regulations that materially affect statements.
	Is managing and utilizing its resources (personnel, property) well and if not, why not?
	Is achieving desired results.
Some General Principles Relating to the GAO's Dictated Expanded Scope	The related concepts are still evolving.

	The audit of a governmental entity may include all or only one or two of the possible four audit scope elements. Engagement letters directed to nonfederal auditors, such as a CPA and state or local government units, should specify the scope elements. Information-gathering assignments—as opposed to audit assignments—should follow standards as much as possible.
IIA Standards. By Definition, Internal Auditing Is an Independent Appraisal Function within an Organization. There are Five General Standards	
Independence	The audit group should be independent of the activities they audit. The audit group's organizational status should be sufficiently high to permit the accomplishment of its responsibility and to be objective.
Professional Proficiency	Due professional care. Adequate staffing with enough technical and educational background. Proper supervision. Compliance with standards of conduct. Staff must possess adequate communication skills.
Scope of Work	Evaluate internal controls. Validate data accuracy. Test compliance with company policy. Ensure that assets are safeguarded. See that economy, efficacy, and program objectives are achieved.

Performance of Audit Work	Audit group is responsible for planning adequate internal audit coverage.
Examining, evaluating, and communicating the results of their reviews.	
Management of Internal Audit Department	The staff must be properly managed with adequate provisions for: Definition of purpose. Planning. Personnel management. Coordination with external auditors. Assurance of quality work.

Index